TESTING: Its Place in Education Today

TESTING

Its Place in Education Today

HENRY CHAUNCEY

President, Educational Testing Service

and JOHN E. DOBBIN

Project Director, Educational Testing Service

HARPER & ROW, PUBLISHERS

NEW YORK, EVANSTON,

AND LONDON

LIBRARY OF CONGRESS CATALOG CARD NUMBER: LC 63-11161

E-T

Contents

Acknowledgments

As is so often the case in preparation of a publication on a technical subject, this book could not have been written without generous help from many people. Although the authors must assume all responsibility for what is said here about tests and testing, those who have contributed to the text by means of critical comments and suggestions cannot be left unmentioned.

For participation in the early planning of this work as well as for critical reading of its later drafts, we are deeply indebted to Anna M. Dragositz, Martin R. Katz, Benjamin Shimberg, and Jane D. Wirsig.

For close scrutiny of and comments on particular chapters, we owe thanks and acknowledgment to Scarvia B. Anderson, William B. Bretnall, William E. Coffman, Matthew T. Downey, Henry S. Dyer, Norman O. Frederiksen, William B. Schrader, Robert E. Smith, and John R. Valley.

For dedication beyond the call of duty in reading and commenting on the book as a whole, we owe special appreciation to J. Thomas Hastings, Richard B. McAdoo, Catherine G. Sharp, William W. Turnbull, and Morey J. Wantman.

We are also indebted to Robert J. Solomon and the test development staff of Educational Testing Service, who prepared the booklet, "Multiple-Choice Questions: A Close Look," which forms the basis for the Appendix in this book.

Finally, we must express our gratitude to Lucy Lawrence Chauncey, whose editorial skill and devotion made the original manuscript into a much more readable book.

HENRY CHAUNCEY
JOHN E. DOBBIN

Princeton, New Jersey
June 1963

vii

Introduction

This book is intended to provide teachers, interested school board members, and parents with a broad picture of what the testing in schools and colleges is all about. It is not a manual, because specific training in testing requires textbooks and courses in measurement. Rather, this is an overview of current educational testing developments, intended to contribute to a general education about education. We hope that it will lead those in the field of education to a more useful understanding of tests and their place in the teaching and learning process.

Many of us who are now professionally active in American education were in school ourselves at some time during the quarter-century between 1925 and 1950. Our common observation is that things have changed. Indeed, things have changed in school, just as they have changed in our government, in the ways we spend our leisure time, and in the goals we set for ourselves and our offspring.

In 1925 the national attitude was one of optimism and of satisfaction with things as they were. Business was good; wages were higher than ever before. More than half of that generation left school and went to work before graduating from high school. Of those who did get through high school, about one in five went on to college. A number of professionals engaged in educational research were working on and trying out new ways of teaching; but schools, by and large, were much the same as they had been since the turn of the century.

By 1935, the whole climate for schools had changed. After six years of deepening economic depression, there were few jobs for boys and girls who quit school; so high school enrollments mushroomed, and the high school curriculum was broadened to offer more vocational courses. The national mind was concentrated on revival of the economy, on WPA, on social security, on the day's groceries.

College enrollments were growing, as the sheer lack of job opportunities forced more young people to keep on going to school until something turned up. Practically anyone who could afford tuition could get in. Educational research was still being carried on, but relatively few people had time to make innovations, because the majority were desperately occupied in hanging on until things got better.

The year 1945 found the America in which our schools did their job altered radically by the war and its demands. Our national attitude had changed. While in 1935 we had been confused, timid, apprehensive, and self-centered as far as our national goals were concerned, by 1945 we collectively had rallied to the cause of human freedom. We had assumed a major role in its defense around the world and had accepted leadership in a world for which freedom had new meanings.

During the war, research was brought out of the ivory tower to bear on the problems of the armed forces in expediting the hasty classification and training of twelve million young men and women; and new methods proved successful. Eighteen-year-olds learned mathematics and physics as if their lives depended on the learning, which was true. Young men learned to speak foreign languages well enough to guide patrols through enemy territory. Thousands who for some reason were unfit for combat were identified and sent away from battle areas.

Colleges and the public attitude toward education were greatly changed by the war. Veterans of Anzio and Kasserine Pass, Normandy and Guadalcanal were aided in enrolling in colleges through the GI Bill. The returning veterans needed counseling to find education, training, and jobs that suited their capabilities, so that there would be no human flotsam on the beachhead of the peace.

The answers to problems of teaching and learning that emerged from the experiences of World War II were not lost on peacetime America. Steadily, if slowly, fresh ideas were adopted and adapted. The dramatic achievements in science and technology made during the 1950s, however, have again shaken up American education and stimulated it into a profusion of new developments. Old subjects are being taught in new and different ways; whole new curriculums are being constructed; language laboratories, television, and techniques ranging from programmed instruction to team teaching are being tried out and improved. At the grass-roots level, school boards are realizing the importance of proper guidance and counseling to enable students to make the best use of their courses and to plan their futures wisely. There is a constant need for evaluation of new methods and programs.

It has become virtually impossible for everyone concerned with education to keep up with all the changes now taking place. Merely assessing the sheer speed and volume of changes directly affecting one's own field of instruction makes it difficult to stay abreast of all the other simultaneous developments. If we could all go to all the meetings and read all the books, there would be no shallow spots in our knowledge of the special fields of education. Nor would there be time for students or classes.

Since there are so many limits to available time, and since students and their needs must have first call on our energies, opportunities to stay informed about a special field such as testing are rare for most teachers, let alone parents. Paradoxically, testing is very much in the public eye and subject to all kinds of commentary—in the press, at school meetings, in periodicals and other media. Certain kinds of tests, such as those for scholarship competition or admission to college, receive public notice comparable to that given to the relocation of the Dodgers or the appointment of the First Lady's dressmaker. Fascinating if garbled accounts of school testing activities or individual test questions are brought home by pupils to their parents.

With so much to know about so many things in an era characterized by rapid and complex change, teachers need sources from which they can acquire accurately the general rationale and pedagogical import of the various educational specializations that relate to instruction. The teacher who cannot become a specialist must still gain enough understanding of a particular field to be able to place it properly in the total spectrum of educational effort and to use its resources constructively and sensibly when the needs arise. This book is intended to be such a source of general information about the tests used in schools and colleges.

TESTING: *Its Place in Education Today*

CHAPTER 1

TESTING
HAS A HISTORY

By the time of the ancient Greeks, the relation of testing to the education of the young was well established and much refined. The Spartans, devoted to physical culture, had an elaborately graduated series of tests through which every boy had to pass in demonstrating his growing mastery of the required skills of manhood. In Athens a more intellectual kind of testing was refined by Socrates to extend and enrich the learning of his pupils—a combination of teaching and testing that is popular in certain fields to this day.

Through the long run of time, those who taught the young also tested them. Teaching was intensely personal. As a rule, the teacher worked with a single pupil, or with a small group of pupils. Under these conditions, testing was a normal part of the give and take of teaching and seldom was regarded as a function separate from teaching.

But times and circumstances changed. Schooling inevitably became more formal as increasing numbers of young people sought an education. The informal class of one to three or four pupils gave way to classes of twenty or thirty pupils per teacher. And this arrangement was generally established practice at the time American education was being organized. The old intimacy was lost. The "teacher" had become the "schoolmaster."

The special problems of teaching created by group instruction were recognized at least as early as the eighteenth century by men concerned about proper education of children. Pestalozzi and Herbart are names as monumental in education as Newton and Darwin in science; for those men saw that even though teachers instructed pupils in groups, they had to understand them as individuals and plan their learning accordingly. What is obvious to us now was an unusual notion two hundred years ago: Students of the same age and approximately the same size do not learn anything at the same rate, in the same sequence, or with the same degree of success, even when they are instructed simultaneously by one teacher. The modern teacher knows that every pupil brings to class his own genes and family background, his own experience, his own interests, his own successes and failures, and his own sense of well-being or lack of it; and that the teacher's instruction is received not by a group but by a collection of quite different individuals.

Tests of Ability

It is difficult to be at the same time brief and fair to the many gifted people who have contributed to the development of psychological and educational testing techniques. For example, Sir Francis Galton and James McKeen Cattell were major figures in the early attempts at measurement of individual differences and in the development of formal testing methods; yet because their work was less directly concerned with the problems of the schools than Alfred Binet's, it is glossed over with no more than passing mention in this condensed history. So, for the sake of brevity, are the contributions of certain later contributors in the field, illustrious men whose place in the history of psychological measurement is well described in the specialized literature of measurement.

In the late 1800s and early 1900s, certain special problems in education engaged the attention of able men in the emerging science of psychology. One of these problems was that of classifying school pupils so that the dullest of them could be identified and separated from the others for special instruction. Psychologists in the United States as well as in Europe had been looking for some time for connections between a child's physical characteristics and his "intelligence," or ability to do school work. Some of the characteristics they measured were size of skull, strength of grip, speed of tapping, speed of reaction, sensitivity to touch, and keenness of vision and hearing. These tests provided no answers, for pupils who were quick to learn in class and those who were slow did about equally well on all of them.

In 1904 the French psychologist Alfred Binet became a member of a commission asked to recommend to the educational authorities of Paris a method for picking out children who were mentally unable to profit from regular school instruction. Having tried to do this job with many of the earlier methods, Binet concluded that more complex tests were needed, tests that would require a child to use the complex mental processes needed in school study and in everyday life. The problems he posed for youngsters were both complex and sensible: Younger children (ages 3–6) were asked to give their family name, to identify familiar objects, to copy figures, to point to their right and left ear, to obey commands. Ten- and eleven-year-olds were asked to name the months of the year in correct order, to recognize and name various coins, to make up sentences in which various key words were provided, to define abstract words, and to arrange scrambled words into a meaningful sentence.

Binet's logic was straightforward. Most children in a given culture, he assumed, are exposed to similar influences. As they grow they have opportunities to learn about themselves and the world in which they live. They develop skill in dealing with everyday problems as well as in solving problems that involve reasoning. So Binet proposed that the degree of brightness in children could be judged by observing their ability to perform correctly tasks similar in nature to those faced in their daily lives.

It is important here to point out a fact that has escaped most laymen. No test or technique measures mental ability directly. What Binet did, and what all other "intelligence test" builders after him have done, was to set up some tasks for the young intellect to attack and then to observe what happened when that intellect was put to work on them. His method was truly scientific and remarkably like the method used by physicists forty years later to detect and measure the forces released by the atom. The cloud chamber does not permit the physicist to see the atom or its electrically charged components, but it does reveal the tracks of ionizing particles and thus permits the scientist to deduce the nature of the atom from which the particles emanate.

Similarly, psychologists cannot peek through a window to assess the quality or power of the mind. All they can do is set up a job for a person's intellect or "intelligence" and then see how well that job is done. If the job is done better or faster than it usually has been done by others of the same age, the tester deduces that this particular intellect is somehow better or stronger than most. If the job is done more poorly or slowly than the average, the tester deduces that this particular intellect is weaker than most, or not experienced in this kind of work, or not properly focused on the job. Tests of intelligence are *work-samples* of a special kind.

Binet's second contribution to measurement of mental ability was his way of describing the differences he found among the intellectual capacities of children. He did this by establishing rough averages of performance among children at successive age levels. But how to describe the children whose performance is not just at the average for their age? Binet's system was simple and is used to this day. To illustrate: If nine-year-old Pierre solved correctly the tasks appropriate for his own age group plus the tasks appropriate for average ten-year-olds and average eleven-year-olds (but encountered trouble with the tasks for average children of twelve years), he was judged to have an intellectual development roughly comparable to that of an average eleven-year-old. Conversely, if nine-year-old Louis was found to be able to handle the tasks for average seven-year-olds but to have great difficulty with tasks for average eight-year-olds, his intellectual development was judged to be comparable to that of an average youngster of seven years.

The measures that Binet and his coworkers developed for estimating mental ability marked the real beginning of modern psychological testing. These measures demonstrated that complex mental processes, processes generally associated with intelligent behavior, could be called forth and evaluated in a systematic way.

The Binet tests were not long in crossing the Atlantic. In 1910, a translation and adaptation was done by Dr. Henry Goddard, director of the training school for retarded children in Vineland, New Jersey. Goddard's enthusiasm for the tests, and their use in early identification of the retarded, encouraged many teachers and others with little or no background in psychology to become "intelligence testers," with the consequence that the newly imported technique often was badly used and earned an unfairly bad press.

At about the same time, Dr. Lewis Terman, at Stanford University, was working on a further adaptation of the Binet tests. He devised new questions, developed new methods for giving and scoring the tests, prepared new norms based on the performance of American children, and wrote a detailed book of instructions for administering the test and interpreting its results. Terman's 1916 test, known as the *Stanford-Binet*, gained wide acceptance and quickly became the standard American "intelligence test." Like Goddard, Terman recognized the usefulness of a test in discovering children who were mentally deficient, but he also saw the potential of such a test for the identification of superior students. His lifelong work with superior children, and his studies of these same children as adults, constitute a major contribution to our understanding of the "gifted" child.

One less fortunate development got its start with the increasing use of the *Stanford-Binet* test, in spite of Terman's word of caution. Other psychologists had developed a simple procedure for expressing the results of a child's performance on the Binet tests as one number. They divided the child's actual age into the age level earned by the child from the number of test questions he could answer successfully—and multiplied the result by 100 to eliminate the decimal point, as shown below.

Chronological Age	Mental Age	Computation	IQ
8 years 0 months	10 years 0 months	$10 \div 8 = 1.25 \times 100$	125
8 years 0 months	6 years 0 months	$6 \div 8 = 0.75 \times 100$	75

This new single-number index (credited by most historians to the German psychologist Wilhelm Stern) was given a name: "intelligence quotient"—IQ for short. It provided a convenient way of summarizing the comparative performance of a child on a given test; if a child's IQ number was substantially less than 100 he had done less well than the average of his age. Terman used this score device for the interpretation of performance on the *Stanford-Binet*, carefully describing it as a convenient "index of brightness" that had a comparison built into it. With the wide acceptance of the *Stanford-Binet* tests, the term IQ came into popular use among teachers and parents very quickly. In a few years, IQ had become synonymous with "intelligence" in the public mind, and the IQ of a child was erroneously assumed to be a permanent and immutable characteristic, like blue eyes or big ears, rather than a score on a particular test at a particular time.

The shortcomings of the IQ in school test score interpretation were the fault of the users far more often than of the index itself. Probably innumerable children were spiritually handicapped, in the heyday of the IQ, by their teachers' or parents' intimation that their low IQ meant they were just plain stupid. Others, proudly inflated by a high score, mistakenly believed they were generally smarter than most anybody. Since other ways of indicating ability in test scores have been developed, and teachers are becoming aware that the IQ is not necessarily a constant number, the era of overinterpretation may be drawing to a close.

For two decades the 1916 edition of the *Stanford-Binet* held a position of outstanding prestige and usefulness. Its use required a trained examiner if its results were to be trusted, and it could be administered to only one child at a time, but it was a tremendously useful tool for the better understanding of individual children and, hence, for better teaching. Beginning in 1926 and working continuously for a full decade, Terman and his associates completely revised the test, introducing changes which experience and research had shown to be necessary. The *Stanford-Binet* in its current version continues to be the most widely used individual test of the mental ability of children in America. Its only major rival is the *Wechsler Intelligence Scale for Children* (WISC), which appeared in 1949. For the individual testing of adolescents and adults, however, the *Wechsler-Bellevue Intelligence Scales,* first published in 1939, appears to have surpassed the *Stanford-Binet* in frequency of use.

Despite their usefulness in schools and clinics, the individual tests of mental ability were too cumbersome and too time-consuming for efficient use with large numbers of people. The limitations were recognized by Terman as well as by other psychologists. Accordingly, one of Terman's students, Arthur Otis, very early began to experiment with methods by which tests of mental ability could be administered to children in groups. Unlike the majority of Binet's and Terman's tests, which required the individual to think of the answer to a question or problem without any clues from the examiner, the test material with which Otis experimented required the subject to pick out the correct answer from among several alternatives provided.

Example: Which one of these five words means the *opposite* of north?
(1) pole   (2) equator   (3) south   (4) east   (5) west

Questions of this kind are called "multiple-choice" questions, for obvious reasons.

When the United States entered World War I, the Army asked the American Psychological Association to help devise a method for classifying recruits rapidly according to their mental ability. A committee headed by Robert Yerkes drew heavily upon Otis's work in developing the group test soon to be known to millions of doughboys—the *Army Alpha Test.* They also devised a group test for illiterates, using drawings and other nonverbal materials, called the *Army Beta Test.* Nearly two million soldiers took the *Army Alpha* in the training camps. This test turned out to be a remarkably good instrument for assigning recruits to jobs with different intellectual demands, for picking out promising officer candidates, and for rejecting those who lacked sufficient mental ability to complete military training successfully.

The period of the twenties and thirties was one of active and painstaking research directed toward improvement in measuring mental ability. If a test that worked well under some circumstances, such as the *Army Alpha,* could not be adapted for other uses and did not perform equally well, then new tests were devised for new situations. Sophisticated techniques—description of score reliability and methods for empirical validation, to name just two—began to come into use.

One of the new improvements was an attempt to separate mental behaviors according to content and by different methods. The earlier tests demonstrated mental functioning as a single, general trait. Measurement of separate and distinct mental functions came into prominence with the work of L. L. Thurstone, at the University of Chicago. He and other psychologists here and abroad led the development of a mathematical method known as multiple factor analysis. By applying this method, they were able to describe the abilities measured by a variety of tests in terms of a fairly small number of "primary mental abilities." This approach led many psychologists to place less emphasis on general intelligence and to think in terms of a number of abilities in describing an individual's strengths and weaknesses.

While the search continues to refine the instruments now used to identify known factors and to isolate new ones, testing of children and students indicates that two clusters or factors of mental ability appear to have a closer relationship with school performance (in terms of marks assigned by teachers) than others yet known. These two are verbal ability—involving vocabulary, sentence understanding, and reading comprehension—and ability in numerical reasoning and computation. Because intelligence of the kind required to succeed in school learning seems to be measured most accurately by tests of verbal and quantitative ability, these kinds of tests are commonly used in schools.

In World War II, for the second time within a generation, the growing techniques for measuring human capacity were brought to bear on problems of national defense. Twelve million men and women were inducted into the armed services, each one assigned to his duty or training at least partly on the basis of his test performance. Mistakes were made, of course. Every veteran recalls or has heard of instances in which individuals were grossly or hilariously miscast in the military drama. Nevertheless, the conversion of twelve million citizen-soldiers into the complex and highly technical force of a modern army was accomplished in time because there were ways of predicting whether a recruit could learn the mathematics of gunnery or would serve the country better driving a supply truck.

One illustration will explain how new techniques of testing were used in the course of World War II. Early in the war, selection of aviation cadets was limited to men with at least two years of college who also were bright, in the sense that they all scored high on tests involving the use of words and numbers. Yet a number of these failed in pilot training. What were the characteristics that separated successful pilots from poor ones, or, for that matter, navigators from bombardiers? How could selection be made more effective?

Dozens of different test ideas were tried out, from paper-and-pencil tests to those indicating the trainee's speed of reaction, his coordination, dexterity, and ability to maintain a steady hand under stress. Many of the trial tests failed to prove useful, but some seemed to show signs of being related to pilot success, and these were analyzed and refined and tried again.

Eventually a large sample of men beginning pilot training was given a trial battery of the most promising tests. No applicant was rejected because of a low score, nor was a high score alone sufficient to keep him on the roster, and the results of the tests were not made known during the trial period.

After the entire group had completed the first stage of pilot training, the test results were studied to see whether there might be any relationship between the individual's test performance and his later success or failure in pilot training. Figure 1 shows the results. Ninety-

FIGURE 1. *Chances of Success in Primary Pilot Training Based on Aptitude Test Scores—185,367 Trainees*

Test Score*	Number of Men	Per Cent Failing Primary Pilot Training
9	21,474	4%
8	19,440	10%
7	32,129	14%
6	39,398	22%
5	34,975	30%
4	23,699	40%
3	11,209	53%
2	2,139	67%
1	904	77%

* This type of score, the "stanine," was devised by the Air Force during World War II and refers to a weighted scale on which 9 represents the highest score and 1 the lowest.

six per cent of the men with the highest scores successfully completed primary training, while 77 per cent of the men who scored lowest "washed out."

The story illustrates the principle most important to an understanding of testing: A test is nothing more than a sample of performance related to the characteristic the examiner is trying to predict or estimate. The Air Force psychologists had to try out many different samples of performance and then wait to see which kinds of test performance were most closely related to later performance in pilot training. This trying-and-waiting procedure is called "validation."

A second important principle is suggested by the results of the Air

Force testing reported in Figure 1. Almost no test or combination of tests has an inherently stable yes-no, pass-fail, go–no-go score. The person who is using the test scores may decide to set a "cutting score" arbitrarily and thus make an artificial pass-fail interpretation of the test results, but the test itself will at best yield a score with a fairly reliable set of probabilities.

At the end of the war, testing had a new military role. The return of twelve million veterans to civilian life during a short span of time quite properly concerned those who cared about individuals and about the nation. A high proportion of these veterans were men who had no vocational training other than military training. Others had left jobs which had changed or disappeared altogether during the war years. Many had interrupted schooling to enter the service and soon would be seeking to press on with their education. Could the country afford to release these millions willy-nilly, without guidance or help, into an economy already struggling with the mammoth conversion back to peacetime operations?

Using personal histories, service records, and tests of ability, of aptitude, of school achievement, and of vocational preparation, the Veterans Administration gathered information to be used in counseling each individual veteran toward the postwar activity or occupation for which he seemed to be best suited. He had only to ask for it, and he received the help of the most thorough, and certainly by far the largest, counseling agency the world had known. With VA support and guidance, millions of veterans left the services to continue education in high schools, colleges, technical schools, and vocational training courses. It has been said that the federal investment in education of veterans after World War II contributed as much to the growth and security of the nation as the military victories earned by these same veterans during the war. In the process of finding and training and using the capacities of people, coming out of military service as well as going into it, tests were used as tools.

Tests of Achievement

Achievement examinations have as long a history as tests of ability. The Spartan youth demonstrated his hard-earned fitness by running to the top of a mountain. The young Athenian scholar successfully engaged other scholars in disputation. And in the United States of a generation ago the pigtailed eighth-grader in the little red schoolhouse stood up and correctly spelled dis-es-tablish-men-tarian-ism at the Friday afternoon "visitation."

The point of the achievement test is to find out whether the student (or soldier or hunter or worker) has learned what the teacher has been trying to teach him. Sometimes the achievement test is aimed at demonstration of a small piece of learning—recall of a single chapter in a book or demonstration of one new stroke in swimming. Other times the achievement test covers a great deal of learning or a complex set of learnings, as in the examinations for admission of a lawyer to the bar. In every case the achievement test calls for a demonstration of learning in some form that can be observed and assessed. Just as in the case of the ability test, the achievement test is a work sample.

From the first schools of early colonial times down to the present, the most frequently used achievement tests have been those prepared by the teacher. And since the major part of school learning for generations has come out of books, it follows that demonstration of learning should be accomplished by speaking and writing.

A step toward standardized testing was introduced by Horace Mann in 1845, when he substituted a uniform written examination for oral interrogation of students by school committeemen in the Boston public schools. Mann's comments about the superiority of the uniform written examination have a curiously modern sound:

1. These examinations are impartial, and there is no possibility of favoritism or "officious interference" by the examiner.
2. Uniform questions eliminate the chance element inherent in oral examinations, where questions vary so widely that the good pupil may miss a hard question while the dullard answers an easy one correctly.
3. Such examinations conserve the time of examiners and permit many questions to be asked of all pupils—the greater the number of questions, the nearer does the examination approach completeness.
4. Uniform examinations place all students under the same conditions —they all run the same race over the same course.

Horace Mann's uniform examinations had one characteristic that was to be of significance in later standardized tests: They required all students to answer the same questions, and a lot of them. Use of the uniform examination is still growing, as school districts, city school systems, and even states, such as New York State with its Regents examinations, have borrowed and adapted the idea.

Probably the first application of a standardized test to an educational problem was accomplished by a physician, J. M. Rice, in 1897. At that time schools were under considerable pressure to add new subjects to the narrowly academic curriculum, and school people generally were countering with a claim that they had too little time to teach the subjects already required. Rice prepared a list of fifty spelling words and administered his test to pupils as he went from town to town. He found little relationship between scores on his "test" and the amount of time a school spent on formal spelling instruction. This simple experiment pointed the way to an objective method for resolving educational differences of opinion.

A giant of the early years of testing was Professor E. L. Thorndike, of Teachers College, Columbia University. Thorndike in 1904 published the first textbook on educational measurement, *An Introduction to the Theory of Mental and Social Measurement,* which is taken by many to mark the beginning of modern times in testing. Thorndike's work was soon followed by other pioneering attempts to measure systematically the outcomes of instruction in various school subjects: In 1908, Stone's arithmetic reasoning test; in 1909, Courtis's arithmetic computation test; in 1910, Thorndike's scale for the handwriting of children; in 1911, the Ayres Handwriting Scale; in 1912, the Hillegas composition scale. The start had been made.

The new aspect of standardized achievement tests was their systematic use of the principles of scientific measurement of human abilities developed in the psychological laboratories. The early workers in the measurement of school achievement carried over from the psychological laboratory a concern for careful control of the conditions of testing and for absolutely objective scoring. Spurring them on in this effort was a series of experiments that showed how unreliable, and often unfair, was the grading of the traditional essay examination.

The educational ferment of the 1920s was basically scientific, in that education generally was shifting from a wholly philosophical base to a position that included scientific self-study. Old ideas were challenged and new ones introduced according to evidence that had been gathered systematically. By 1915 specialists with responsibility for educational research were numerous enough to form a professional organization. Early in the twenties more than one hundred bureaus of educational research were established in large city school systems, in state departments of education, and in state universities.

Many professional articles on testing and applications of testing in educational research began to appear. New educational and psychological journals were established in response to growing activity in these fields. Books on statistical methods for use in educational research were published. Publishers previously engaged in the preparation of textbooks added technicians to their staffs and began the commercial publication of standardized tests. And since the major focus of all this effort was on measuring what and why and how young people learn in school, tests were built and printed or mimeographed by practically everyone who had an interest in the problem—teachers, researchers, psychologists, professors of education, book publishers, graduate students.

The wholesale building of tests in the 1920s had several results. On the good side was the encouragement that testing gave to teachers to re-examine their teaching goals and to think over again the content of their instruction. Also on the good side was the general acceptance of testing, created by the widespread public interest and the multitude of amateur test-builders, which made it possible for the little group of trained professionals in the field to carry on the large tryouts necessary for the building of real standardized tests. A landmark in the history of educational measurement was the publication, in 1923, of the first *Stanford Achievement Test,* a "battery" of standardized achievement tests in elementary school subjects— developed by L. M. Terman (builder of the *Stanford-Binet*), T. L. Kelley, and G. M. Ruch. This test, and the methods used to produce it, foreshadowed many characteristics of modern testing.

On the debit side of the early enthusiasm for testing, the list of effects is longer. Most of the tests put together by eager amateurs and hawked among their colleagues were not very good, and they soured a lot of teachers on the whole idea of testing. Almost without exception, the amateur-made tests measured only recall of specific subject matter content, asking only for regurgitation of the text; so teachers and parents came to feel that all tests covered only a small part of what schools were attempting to teach. Many people grew to think that all objective tests were true-false tests (as many of the slapped together instruments of the period were).

The most detrimental effect of the early enthusiasm for tests was the disenchantment produced by exaggerating the benefits of tests and overinterpreting their results. Educators and public alike had been oversold on educational testing. When it began to appear that tests did not measure as much or as accurately as their enthusiasts claimed, there was a reaction against school testing—a reaction that persists in some forms to this day.

The leaders among the professionals continued with their work—trying new approaches, refining ideas, and running experimental try-outs; and the number of such professionals grew. Teachers College at Columbia University led all others in the number of scholars and researchers devoted to psychological and educational measurement. Other centers of educational thought, too, began in this period to develop leadership in measurement—Stanford, Chicago, Peabody, and Iowa among them. Researchers in the older field of experimental psychology crossed over now and then to the applied problems of education; and still other centers of leadership grew in the emerging "science" of measuring and predicting how people learn: the universities of Harvard, Michigan, Ohio State, Yale, Minnesota, and Princeton, to name just a few.

The first *Stanford Achievement Test* foreshadowed several things to come in the preparation of standardized tests for school use. This elementary school test battery of 1923 stood out over the welter of unsubstantial tests of its time for these reasons: (1) It was built by a group of highly trained professionals working as a team; (2) its content was drawn from a survey of many different courses of study, so that its questions were representative of what was being taught in all parts of the country; (3) its questions were tried out experimentally, to see how well they worked, before they were used in a final test form; and (4) the final test forms were given to thousands of school children in many different school systems to obtain comparative samples of performance (norms). This long, difficult, and expensive process requires the effort of many people and the investment of considerable sums for years before the investment can be recovered through sale of the finished tests.

Publication of this battery of tests brought together in a joint risk venture, for the first time, the combination of resources necessary for development of good standardized tests: a team of professionals in measurement, the help of educators all over the country, an established publisher, and capital to support the venture until the tests could be sold. The *Stanford Achievement Test* proved to be extremely useful to elementary school people in assessing the academic learning of their students; millions of copies were sold, and the original investment was returned. Test publication had passed from an amateur to a professional basis, and the general characteristics of the publication process had been established.

Tests of school achievement are as varied as they are numerous. Most of the earlier ones, and many of the tests now used, measure little more than recall of factual information. There are two reasons for this: (1) Learning and retention of factual information is an important purpose of school instruction, and (2) measurement of other kinds of learning (insights, understandings, attitudes, points of view) is much more difficult to accomplish. But even in the measurement of factual recall, tests are different, one from another, because any school achievement test is just a sample of the things a student is taught. Every test-maker draws on a different sample of learning when he frames his questions.

The limitation of early achievement tests to measurement of recall was recognized from the outset by the professionals in the field. To go beyond the recall or recognition of facts and measure other learnings—the ability to gather information and draw conclusions, for example, or the habit of suspending judgment until information has been obtained—is more difficult. But it was attempted, again and again, by those who wanted to encourage good teaching by providing tests of the harder-to-measure outcomes of good teaching.

A number of promising leads were developed in the direction of testing the broader outcomes of teaching, but three particular efforts, each supported by large resources, will be mentioned here: the Pennsylvania Study, begun in the late 1920s, supported by the Carnegie Foundation for the Advancement of Teaching; the Eight-Year Study of the 1930s, sponsored by the Progressive Education Association; and the Study of General Education (college level) of the 1940s, supported by the American Council on Education. Each of these efforts was partly based upon previous research and each added something important to the techniques of measuring school learning. One enormous contribution of the men who led these researches was development of a rationale and a vocabulary with which they could explain what they were trying to do. The general conclusions might be paraphrased as follows:

The purpose of schools is to educate each young person in such a way that he will be able, to the limits of his natural ability, to contribute to the welfare and strength of American society and to realize a full development of his own potential as a human being. In order to do this, the school teaches each child certain subject matter content, such as English and history and mathematics, so that he may have the knowledge with which to solve his problems; the learning of this content is the immediate goal of instruction. When he has learned some subject matter and mastered some skills, the school teaches the student to apply them in a variety of new situations, so that he will be able to use them when they are needed in nontextbook circumstances; learning to use school-learned knowledge in a variety of ways is the intermediate goal of instruction. When he knows the subject matter and how to apply it, the ultimate goal of the school is that he will apply his learning, bettering his own life and the lives of his fellows.

This is a set of ideas that makes education easier to study and assess. Successful achievement of the ultimate goals of schooling depends on successful achievement of the intermediate goals, which, in turn, depends on the learnings that make up the immediate goals. With this definition, it became clear that achievement tests in subject matter had now reached the point of evaluating how well students attain the immediate goals of instruction. With continued refinement, the direction of the next step in testing was clear—toward measurement of abilities to apply knowledge, the intermediate goals.

A useful application of the new concept was developed by the United States Armed Forces Institute during World War II. With millions of young people in service who wanted somehow to continue their interrupted educations, the Armed Forces Institute set into motion a gigantic program of correspondence courses, in which servicemen enrolled all over the world. The Institute developed tests by which veterans could gain credit for courses taken in service in obtaining high school diplomas or getting into college. How could they equate the physics learned after hours in a supply depot with the physics learned by demonstration and lecture in a classroom? Or ancient history read by flashlight in a dugout with ancient history studied in a hushed library?

USAFI sought the answers by measurement of the intermediate goals of instruction in these subjects; they built tests which attempted to measure the student's understanding of the principles of the subject and his ability to use these principles in the solution of new problems, regardless of the source or nature of his instruction. The product of this USAFI effort was the series of tests called Tests of General Educational Development. By arrangement with thousands of high schools and hundreds of colleges, these tests were used to bring veterans back into formal schooling with full credit for their wartime learning. The work of USAFI and its acceptance by civilian educators constitute one of the most satisfying episodes, in terms of the conservation of human talent, in the history of education. The tests built by USAFI have been models for test improvement ever since.

Measuring the achievement of the ultimate goals of education is something else again. One can test students on their knowledge of the facts of local government (immediate goal) and their ability to apply this knowledge to different kinds of problems (intermediate goal), but it has not yet been possible to test them ten years after they are out of school to find out whether any sizable unit of education—say, a college major in political science—has contributed more to the personal fulfillment or social effectiveness of young people than an equivalent amount of time and effort spent in travel or apprenticeship.

Measuring Student Interests

It is axiomatic that good teaching often depends on the ability of the teacher to ascertain the interests of the learner, as well as his capacities, and to capitalize upon them. Good teachers and counselors often use an individual's special interests as means for reinforcing learning or awakening motivation to learn. For this reason, tests and inventories for discovery of students' interests have been used in schools for many years.

The oldest and best known of the standardized interest inventories used in schools is the *Strong Vocational Interest Blank,* one form for men and the other for women, which had its origins in early research done at Carnegie Institute of Technology. Work on the inventory was continued by its author, E. K. Strong, Jr., while he was at Stanford University. The inventory has been in school use since 1927. Through many revisions and countless research applications, the *Strong Vocational Interest Blank* has built up a body of background information that permits a good counselor in high school or college to help a student in recognizing and interpreting his interests. With the proper administration and interpretation of this inventory, it is possible for a student to discover whether his interests are similar to those of sales managers, of physicists, or of musicians. Such a discovery of shared interest means a great deal to young people who are at that lonely point in the maturation process at which one must decide on directions in which life must turn.

Another inventory of interests related to occupational fields is the *Kuder Preference Record,* which appeared in its original form in 1934. This instrument, too, can be used to help students understand their own interests in the light of how those interests may relate to various occupations.

There are several other inventories of interests used in schools, but the *Strong* and the *Kuder* are both the ancestors and the prototypes of all others concerned with interest and vocation. Both have long histories of research. Both have survived a period in which users with more enthusiasm than information overinterpreted their results.

No standardized inventory or combination of inventories—of interests or of any other attributes—will tell an individual student that he should become a doctor, or an artist, or anything else. Properly used, such an inventory can add one more bit of evidence that may be helpful to him in making up his mind about vocational goals to pursue, but it cannot tell him what he should do. This much has been learned by school people and most parents since the advent of interest inventories; its recognition is an event of some note in the history of measurement.

Measuring Personal Characteristics

Teachers and parents have been interested in the testing of "personality" for as long as they have been interested in the testing of

academic achievement. Many human beings are rather more interested in hanging a personality label on other people than in achieving
a deeper understanding of themselves. What is lacking is a method
for observing and describing personality that is as objective and accurate as description of physical or intellectual characteristics. Psychologists have long been striving to develop such a method. Progress has
been painfully slow. The nature of the individual personality is even
more difficult to perceive than the nature of intellect. Although there
are several different major theories about formation of the individual
personality structure, all theories rely on observation of individual
reaction to certain factors of environment, natural or artificial, to
provide evidence about the nature of a personality. A great deal of
research has been undertaken in the field, but there is not yet available for general use in schools any test that will describe or categorize
the personality of normal people with the accuracy of academic
ability and achievement tests.

Programs of Testing for Selection

All of the major selection testing programs operate to make the
competition for college admissions more equitable, to help students
get into the right college, and to assist them in locating scholarship
aid. The oldest and best known of these programs is run by the College Entrance Examination Board, an association of over five hundred colleges with additional representatives from secondary schools.
The College Board examination program was started at the turn of
the century as the result of a proposal that colleges requiring examinations for admission would do both the high schools and the applicants a service by setting a common examination on which an
applicant could earn admission to any of a number of colleges. Until
the College Board was formed, a student who wanted to enter his
application at three colleges had to take three different examinations
at three different times and places. The principal of any high school
that had many college-going graduates had an exasperating time trying to arrange for and comply with the multitude of examinations his
seniors needed to take in order to apply to their various college
choices, not to mention preparing the students for the examinations.

A major change occurred in the American educational culture in the fifteen years following World War II. This change was first seen as a mushrooming of the college population and was the result of several forces acting together. The GI Bill brought college education within reach of thousands of veterans who would not have considered going to college without its assistance, and thereby set a "college-going" example in families where it had not existed. The average individual income rose to new highs and stayed there, making a college education possible for youngsters whose parents could not have afforded it a generation earlier, while the technology of business and industry grew at such a furious rate and to such heights of complexity that "Help Wanted" pages were filled with attractive positions for young people requiring at least some college training. The college-educated person had become the object of greater respect in the popular eye, and college education had become more desirable to more people for personal reasons. All together, these forces swamped many colleges with applicants.

In addition to the rapidly growing program of the College Board, several more testing programs, national or regional in scope and focused also on young people in transition between high school to college, were developed in the 1950s. The Westinghouse Talent Search, launched earlier, reached across the country. The Selective Service Examinations provided for draft deferment of able students. Then came other tests for selection of students for scholarship awards —the General Motors Scholarships, the hundreds of private, industrial, and philanthropic scholarships, and, largest of all, the National Merit Scholarships. In 1959, the American College Testing Program was established to screen applicants to colleges which did not use the College Board program.

Thus in a period of sixty years educational testing has developed from a part-time chore of psychologists to a set of techniques that affects every student in school and college. The history of testing has been one of dedicated effort by a great many people to shape and sharpen and wield a tool that can be of great help to educators everywhere.

CHAPTER 2

TESTS
OF LEARNING ABILITY

In their school use, "intelligence tests" and "scholastic aptitude tests" have exactly the same purpose—to estimate the capacity of the student for school learning—and often are called by the more accurate general name that fits both of them: "tests of learning ability." However, though their purpose is the same, tests of intelligence and tests of scholastic aptitude differ somewhat in content, in interpretation, and, very roughly, in the levels of maturity at which they are used.

Intelligence Tests

A significant point about all intelligence tests is that they measure only the individual's capacity for learning. No intelligence test opens a window in the student's skull through which psychologists can ascertain the amount of latent brightness or intelligence he has. Nor can any test trick a person, psychologically or otherwise, into revealing how much brilliance or stupidity he possesses. A rough appraisal of the individual's comparative capacity for learning is the most that the best test of intelligence can provide.

A second characteristic of intelligence tests is that the intelligence test confronts the student with tasks on which he can demonstrate his skills for learning, and then compares his work with the work of others on the same tasks. The basic idea is that of the work-sample. The intelligence test is no more than a standard job on which students can demonstrate their learning speed and skill.

A third important characteristic of intelligence tests is that they do not measure purely innate ability. Said another way, intelligence tests measure mental ability in terms of something that has already been learned. If there is in human beings a pure mental force, a latent power to perform mental tasks transmitted in the genes and born with the individual, it has not yet been isolated or measured. Scientists suspect that such a pure power does exist, for—like the physicists inquiring into the nature of the atom—they can "see its tracks"; even among tiny infants there are differences in the behavior of adapting to environment that cannot be explained wholly by the environment itself. But even though "native intelligence" is suspected to exist, the intelligence tests we use in this generation measure not innate ability but a developed ability in which innate ability and learned behavior are mixed in unknown proportions.

Some experimental work has been accomplished in reducing the effects of environment on intelligence test performance. In order to obtain a more realistic estimate of the mental abilities of children handicapped by a deprived environment, for example, tests have been devised with content less dependent on experience in the "average" cultural environment. These special tests of mental ability, called "culture-free tests of intelligence" or "culture-fair tests," are still largely in an experimental state. All tests of intelligence used in our schools are used to predict success in our schools as they are. In a school for hunting, fishing, and fighting among Australian aborigines, prediction of success at such learning would require different work-samples than our intelligence tests; but "intelligence tests" they would be.

A fourth important characteristic of intelligence tests is that the estimates of learning capacity they provide are always comparative. That is, no intelligence test yields a measure of learning capacity or "intelligence" in absolute units like quarts or centimeters or ohms. Rather, the intelligence test (like almost all other tests used in education) only tells whether a particular student has done better or worse than a number of other students on the same learning jobs—and, within gross limits, how much better or worse.

To describe the nature and content of several tests used widely in schools, we can begin with tests used with very young children and work up the age scale to tests used with adults.

Very young children (less than five or six years) always are tested by individual intelligence tests (the examiner testing one child at a time in a place away from other children), so that the examiner can be sure that directions are understood and can observe the child as he attempts the test tasks. Although there are half a dozen or more carefully made tests for infants and children of preschool age, the most widely used tests of this kind for young children are the *Merrill-Palmer Scale* and the *Minnesota Preschool Scale*. The *Merrill-Palmer Scale* includes relatively few language tasks, most of the tasks being of the performance type. The language tasks include memory span for words and meaningful word groups, answers to simple questions (e.g., "What does a doggie say?"), and action-association kinds of questions (e.g., "What runs?" "What cries?"). The performance tasks include such things as throwing a ball, standing on one foot, buttoning, folding paper, fitting cubes into a box. Some involve matching colors or pictures, reconstructing cut-out picture puzzles, and copying drawings. A principal characteristic of the *Merrill-Palmer Scale* is its appeal to young children, a consequence of the nature of the tasks as well as the attractiveness of brightly colored materials, an appeal that makes it relatively easy for young children to become sufficiently involved really to perform in the test situation. The *Merrill-Palmer Scale,* as do all other tests for preschool children, requires administration by an examiner trained and experienced in its use. It is worth noting that this test and others for preschool children call upon the child to demonstrate skills and knowledge he has already learned.

Of the available individual tests of intelligence for children in the early school ages, the *Stanford-Binet Intelligence Scale* and the *Wechsler Intelligence Scale for Children* (WISC) are by far the most frequently used. The *Stanford-Binet* at this level mixes "verbal items" (those requiring an understanding of language) with "performance items" (problems not involving or stressing use of language) and yields one total score. At the six-year level, the following are some of the kinds of tasks that have appeared in the *Stanford-Binet* (drawn from the 1937 edition):

1. *Vocabulary*. The child is asked the meaning of words from a graded list of forty-five terms. Credit is given (at this level) for five correct definitions.

2. *Copying a bead chain from memory*. The child is asked to make a chain like the examiner's. Credit is given if all beads are placed correctly.

3. *Mutilated pictures*. The child is shown five pictures in which an object has a missing part and is asked to say what is missing in each. Credit is given for getting four problems correct.

4. *Number concepts*. The child is asked to hand different numbers of blocks to the examiner. Credit is given for selecting the correct number of blocks three times out of four trials.

5. *Pictorial likenesses and differences*. The child is shown six cards with a number of pictorial figures on each. The child is asked to point out the figure that is different. Credit is given for five correct responses out of six.

6. *Maze tracing*. The child is shown three designs, each of which shows two ways for a person to get home. One route of each pair is longer than the other. The child is asked to trace the shorter route. Credit is given for two correct responses out of three.

(Again, the child's success depends largely on some previous learning.)

The *Wechsler Intelligence Scale for Children*, published as a downward extension of the *Wechsler-Bellevue Intelligence Scales*, has come into wide use with children of school age. The WISC cannot be used with children of preschool age, or with severely retarded youngsters in the primary grades, but has some advantages over the *Stanford-Binet* with normal or bright pupils in the primary grades and with all pupils in middle and upper grades—in part because the WISC provides separate scores on verbal material and performance tasks.

The WISC content is composed of the following kinds of subtests:

Verbal Scale	*Performance Scale*
1. General information	6. Picture completion
2. General comprehension	7. Picture arrangement
3. Arithmetic	8. Block design
4. Similarities	9. Object assembly
5. Vocabulary (alternate: Digit span)	10. Coding (alternate: Mazes)

Because the WISC, with its performance IQ as one of two scores, makes it possible to obtain more accurate estimates of mental abilities of youngsters with language handicaps or foreign backgrounds, this test is gaining in popularity over the *Stanford-Binet* in the age span it covers. The *Stanford-Binet* is used more than all other instruments combined in the mental testing of younger school-age children and is still the "old stand-by," but the *Wechsler Intelligence Scale for Children* has surpassed it in frequency of use with older children.

To reiterate, however, a test can be no better than its user; so a school's choice between these two good instruments usually is based on the training, experience, and preference of the examiner who will do the testing. A good examiner, well trained and long experienced with either one of these tests, can obtain a more dependable estimate of learning capacity than a poorly trained or inexperienced examiner with the other test. In both tests the child is asked to perform certain standard intellectual tasks under the guidance of the examiner. The examiner watches that performance intently, making judgments about it. Only after professional instruction and a long internship, including considerable experience under supervision, is an examiner qualified to make the judgments necessary to use the individual intelligence test. This is not a job for the amateur or the self-trained.

The developing intellectual processes of children are more accessible to psychological tests between the ages of two and five than they are in infancy, but the problem of measuring with any accuracy is still acute. While infants do little to indicate their mental abilities, the preschool child sometimes does too much. He is so active and distractable—or so very shy with a stranger—that the examiner must be extremely skillful, and lucky, to obtain a dependable test performance. A safe general conclusion is that below the age at which the child can read fairly well, an intelligence test score is considerably less dependable than it is when he is older. That is, two different testings of the same child younger than five years are likely to produce quite different results. In fact, intelligence test scores obtained with children in kindergarten and grades one and two are none too dependable.

When a child enters school and approaches formal group instruction for the first time, a real need for estimating his mental development appears. It has been known for centuries, of course, that some children insist on learning to read when they are no more than four years old, while other children within that long range of ability called "normal" cannot really read until they are eight or nine. Psychologists are more or less agreed that formal instruction by conventional methods in reading and arithmetic is rather futile before a child reaches a "mental age" of about six—which is to say that stage of mental development and experience characteristic of the average of children who are six years old by the calendar.

Knowing which children are mentally developed enough to undertake formal instruction and which children need to accumulate more of the experience needed to make them ready for formal instruction is one of the important jobs of the kindergarten and primary-grade teachers. It is important because the child who is ready to read and is denied the opportunity develops bad habits ("school is for dopes") and often becomes the disciplinary terror of the classroom, while the child who is forced to read when he is not ready for it in mental skill and experience builds defenses against learning (the process has humiliated him in his first contact with it) that may get in his way for years.

Children of school age are tested much more often with group tests of intelligence than with individual tests. In a group test the child generally indicates his response to directions or to a problem by making a pencil mark on a printed test page. With children in the primary grades, the group test usually is given to very small groups, ten or twelve children at a time, so that the examiner may be able to direct, encourage, and control them more effectively. The examiner often is the teacher. The group test is used in preference to the individual test because it requires fewer hours of testing time for the examiner (one hour, say, to test a dozen pupils, compared with one hour to test each pupil) and less training on the part of the examiner. In many schools, use of the individual intelligence test and the trained examiner it requires is limited to special cases—to children who are suspected of being unable to cope with the group tests and unlikely to earn a dependable score on them.

What are group tests of intelligence like? In the primary grades, these tests require the child neither to read nor to write, but only to follow directions given orally and supported by gestures as he looks at materials that are wholly graphic. Illustrative problems from the *Pintner-Cunningham Primary Test* are:*

Examiner says—

1. Mark the things that Mother uses to sew her apron

   (Picture of scissors, coffeepot, thimble, skillet, needle, kettle, cup, and spool of thread)

2. Mark the two things that belong together

   (Picture of hat, coat, saucepan, hammer)

3. Mark the things that go up in the air

   (Picture of turtle, cat, cow, butterfly, rabbit, airplane, dog, bee, kite, pig, bird, etc.)

Notice that these illustrative problems, drawn from a test for children in kindergarten and the first half of first grade, require the child to call upon his experience in order to solve new problems and see new relationships. Other group intelligence tests used at the primary grade level follow this general pattern.

At the level of the elementary grades, where most children have at least some reading skill, the group tests of intelligence change in their character and content from the concrete pictorial materials used in the first grades to more abstract symbolism, written language, and numbers. For example, the ability to see relationships among things and ideas is sampled this way in the first grade: The examiner says, "Look at the row of pictures and mark the picture that shows what goes with a cat the way a worm goes with a robin"; and the child finds and marks the picture of the mouse in a row that contains pictures of a cat, a dog, a cat in bed, and a mouse. At the fourth-grade level, the same kind of ability is sampled in a problem that is contained wholly on the printed page and has no oral directions by the examiner:

Mark the word which has the SAME or most nearly the same meaning as the first word.

Correct (a) neat (b) fair (c) right
(d) poor (e) good

* Quoted with permission of the publisher, Harcourt, Brace & World, Inc.

Choose the word which is OPPOSITE, or most nearly opposite, in meaning to the first word.

North   (a) hot   (b) east   (c) west
          (d) down   (e) south

Circle the number in this series that is wrong.
1 — 2 — 4 — 8 — 14 — 16 — 32

What would be the NEXT set of five numbers in this series?
3 4 5 6 7   7 3 4 5 6   6 7 3 4 5   _____

The ability to see relationships, in both verbal and quantitative materials as well as in ideas represented by pictures, is sampled in one way or another by every intelligence test used in schools. Hence, in nearly every intelligence test at the level of the middle grades there is an opposites test and an analogies test among the verbal materials and a number completion test and a number sequence test among the quantitative materials.

All of the intelligence tests used in the elementary grades and junior high school set up several different kinds of tasks on which the student is to demonstrate his learning skill. These different tasks do not have the same names in tests made by different publishers—in fact, no two tests by different authors are exactly alike in any respect—but examination of a number of them indicates a general similarity in concept. There are tasks of a verbal kind: knowledge of the meaning of words, seeing relationships among words, understanding ideas expressed in words. Then there are test tasks of a numerical kind: manipulating numbers in computation, seeing relationships among ideas expressed in numbers, understanding logical sequences in numbers, and solving number problems. There often are tasks that combine verbal and numerical content, so as to set up problems in "reasoning" for the student. And, finally, there are tasks on which the student can demonstrate his mental keenness with materials that are neither verbal nor numerical, but concerned with ability to do such things as perceive relationships among shapes or to rearrange the scattered parts of geometric patterns. A person's capacity for dealing with problems of this sort is spoken of as "spatial ability."

Although the intelligence tests most widely used in the elementary and junior high school grades have much in common as far as their content is concerned, they differ dramatically in the interpretations of performance they offer. It is this very great diversity of interpretation that has contributed much to the layman's confusion about intelligence tests. For example, the *Kuhlmann-Anderson Tests,* which have the word "intelligence" in their title everywhere except on the materials the student will see, contain ten different short subtests of the various kinds mentioned in the paragraphs above; but the student earns a single score—an IQ—on the basis of the average of his performance (his median score) on all ten subtests. This, then, is a generalized intelligence quotient score reflecting the individual's average skill on many different but unspecified tasks.

The single-score IQ interpretation provided by the *Kuhlmann-Anderson Tests* is characteristic also of several other intelligence tests much used in schools—the *Otis Quick-scoring Mental Ability Tests* and the *Henmon-Nelson Tests of Mental Ability,* to mention just two. The single-score IQ interpretation of test performance resembles very much the interpretation that Binet gave to performance on his early tests of school-learning ability, and is convenient to use when the user understands its full meaning; but it also has contributed to the general misapprehension that intelligence is unitary and can be measured by a single test and represented by a single number.

The *California Test of Mental Maturity (Short Form)* also has content of the various kinds mentioned, but it provides a different interpretation of performance. Four subscores are reported on a profile: spatial relationships, logical reasoning, numerical reasoning, and verbal concepts. Then the scores on verbal materials are added together to yield a "language IQ," and the nonverbal scores are summed to yield a "nonlanguage IQ." There is also a total IQ, computed from performance on all tasks in the test. The purpose of this multiple IQ interpretation is that of noting the youngster whose overall IQ score may have been depressed by language handicaps such as a deficiency in reading skill or a foreign language background. At any rate, this is a widely used intelligence test that gives not one but three IQ scores.

The *SRA Primary Mental Abilities Test* is yet another intelligence test used in many schools. And it offers yet another kind of interpretation of performance. A percentile rank score is provided for performance on each of seven different subtests—verbal meaning, space, reasoning, number, word fluency, memory, and perceptual speed—

and an IQ is provided for the total. The manual for this test urges the interpreter to use the over-all IQ score as a general estimate of learning capacity, rather than as a specific index, and to give relatively more attention to the student's percentile rank scores on the subtests (percentile rank scores are discussed in Chapter 3).

So, in glancing only briefly at several of the best and most widely used intelligence tests, we see that performance—though always comparative—is described in several different ways: as a single or general IQ score, as verbal and nonverbal IQ scores, as percentile scores on certain factors of intelligence. Not quite so evident is the fact that IQ scores themselves, when used, are computed in at least two different ways. One is the original Binet-type IQ, in which the test performance is given an average "mental age" value and is divided by the student's actual chronological age. The other is a "deviation IQ," which is computed by a more sophisticated method that takes into account the performance of all pupils on a test (mean of 100, with one standard deviation in the norming group arbitrarily equal to 15 IQ points).

These differences in the interpretation of performance on intelligence tests are mentioned not to suggest that one is better than another, but to highlight the fact that no person can have "an" IQ label as the consequence of taking an intelligence test. If he takes such a test, he may earn an IQ score on it, but that IQ score reflects nothing more nor less than his performance on the test he took, at the time he took it.

Because the various intelligence tests used in schools measure generally the same kinds of intellectual skills and experience, a student whose performance earns a high score on one test usually is expected to earn a high score on another test. Similarly, the student who earns a very low score on one test, all other things being equal, probably will earn a low score on a second but different test. But in neither case would the student be expected to earn the same score on both tests. There is enough difference in test content, in method of score interpretation, and in the composition of the publisher's "norming sample" of the population—from test to test—to make the earning of identical IQ scores on two different intelligence tests sheer accident. And there is enough variation in the student himself from day to day (we all have our good and bad days) to make it very unlikely that he will earn exactly the same IQ score if he retakes the same test.

Only a few intelligence tests used with adults yield IQ scores. The IQ was used with adults more frequently some years ago and led to the startling conclusion that people level off in their intellectual capacity after the age of about sixteen and begin a long decline after twenty-one. This unlikely notion somehow gained wide acceptance among the general public. From evidence now available, it is clear that the average adult continues to develop in his ability to learn some kinds of things until middle or later life.

The IQ score does not work as well with adults as it does with children in school because schoolish kinds of learning are replaced by other kinds of learning not related to the test, and also because the comparison, or norming, group with which an individual is compared becomes diffuse; that is, all twelve-year-olds may be somewhat alike in their previous learning experiences (they have had only twelve years in which to become different from one another), but how much alike would any group of forty-year-olds be? For these reasons, most intelligence tests used with adults today are interpreted in terms of a direct comparison, such as percentile rank, with other individuals in a carefully described group, as: This score is higher than the scores earned by 70 per cent of a group of 314 lawyers successfully engaged in private practice. One of the privileges of an adult these days is being too old to have an IQ.

Scholastic Aptitude Tests

Intelligence tests and scholastic aptitude tests have the same purpose: to estimate the capacity of the student for school learning. The two kinds of tests overlap considerably in their content and in the nature of the intellectual tasks they require the student to perform. It is only for the sake of simplifying the discussion that intelligence tests and scholastic aptitude tests are treated separately here. For all practical purposes, and in all of their school uses, they are the same kind of test.

One difference in content is characteristic of the scholastic aptitude test alone. Whereas the intelligence tests generally are composed of verbal tasks, numerical tasks, and often some other kinds of tasks that are neither verbal nor numerical but have to do with space perception or recognition of ideas represented by figures—"nonacademic" skills—the scholastic aptitude tests include verbal and numerical content but omit the nonacademic tasks. In other words, the intelligence tests have two-thirds to three-fourths of their content devoted to skills directly taught in school; the academic or scholastic aptitude tests have all of their content devoted to skills taught in school. Descriptions of the content of two such tests will serve to illustrate.

The *School and College Ability Test* (SCAT), as its name implies, is a measure of academic ability. Various forms of it are used in school all the way from fourth grade through college. It contains four subtests, two verbal and two numerical. The verbal tests are (1) sentence completion tasks that are short reading comprehension jobs and (2) a vocabulary test. The numerical tests are (1) an arithmetic computation test and (2) an arithmetic problem-reasoning test. The two verbal subtests together yield a verbal score, the two arithmetic subtests together yield a quantitative score, and all four yield a total score.

The *Scholastic Aptitude Test* (SAT), the selection test administered for college admission purposes by the College Entrance Examination Board, is three hours long. It yields two scores, verbal and mathematical. The verbal score is based on several kinds of questions, usually antonyms, sentence completions, analogies, and reading comprehension. The mathematical score is based on material which permits the student to demonstrate (1) how well he has mastered elementary mathematics and (2) how well he can apply what he already knows to new situations. The two scores of the SAT are not added together to make a total score, but are always considered separately in predicting how well a student is likely to do at a particular college.

Some scholastic aptitude tests, widely used with considerable success in predicting the academic learning achievements of students, are almost wholly verbal. The *Ohio State University Psychological Test* is one of these. So is the *Miller Analogies Test,* used mostly in the guidance and selection of graduate students. These measures are almost wholly verbal not because the mathematical factor does not add to the accuracy of prediction, but because the single best predictor of success in most college courses is the student's performance on a job that involves use of words and ideas. This fact is a reasonable one when you recall that the earning of a good grade in most college work depends on ability to read, to listen, to write, and to understand the relationships among ideas expressed in words. A mathematical test sharpens the prediction of success in some mathematics courses, but a verbal test is related to the skills needed to succeed in nearly all college courses.

In general, then, the work-samples that are called "intelligence tests" usually contain some work materials related to skills not learned in school, sometimes yield a performance score that is called an IQ, and are used more often in the primary and elementary grades than in high school or college. The work-samples that are called "scholastic aptitude tests," on the other hand, usually contain work materials that are all related to skills learned in school, usually yield a comparative score other than an IQ, and are used more often in high school and college than in the lower grades. Both kinds of tests, regardless of their names, are work-samples rather than windows on the mind and are used to help the teacher understand the pupil well enough to teach him.

Using the Tests of Learning Abilities

John Dewey, the philosopher whose works have been criticized most sharply by people who have never read them, once said, "You might as well say you have 'sold' when no one has bought, as say you have 'taught' when no one has learned." Whether they agree with Dewey's pedagogical principles or not, most teachers have some concern for the capacity of students to learn what they have to teach. And in this concern lies the reason for using tests of learning ability.

The traditionally accepted purpose of teaching in the primary and elementary grades is that of training every child to use the tools of learning—reading, writing, using numbers. Though there are discussions of and disagreements on how these tools of learning may be taught best to all children, there is full agreement that they should be taught, both in preparation for higher levels of schooling and for their necessary uses in day-to-day living. Instruction in the three R's may no longer be the primary teacher's only responsibility, but it remains her first responsibility.

The central learning task in all of the three R's is mastery of symbolism—letters, words, and numbers that symbolize things and ideas. Every normal child comes to school with some symbolic learning already mastered. In order for the teacher to give each child appropriate learning help, she has to know where he is located currently on the long ladder of symbolic learning, and then help him to go on from there. To assist her in the locating job, she uses the learning ability test.

The good primary teacher has access to many kinds of evidence about readiness to learn. She sees the child every school day, talks with him about the many things a child thinks of to talk about, watches him at play and at work with his classmates, accepts his confidences, and observes the child in a whole variety of circumstances. From these observations the teacher draws tentative conclusions about his personal and social maturity, about the depth and richness of his background for school learning, about his readiness for formal instruction in reading and number work. His performance on a group intelligence test adds a comparative and objective observation of him.

A collection of information about each child develops year by year and is increasingly valuable to teachers in understanding that child's learning background and potential. Teachers in second and third grades read the recorded observations of the teachers ahead of them, talk with those teachers about particular children, make their own additional observations, and often administer the learning ability tests again at the beginning of each year—both to confirm or modify previous findings and to keep track of changes that occur as the child develops his skill in "schoolmanship."

In the middle school grades (4–5–6), learning ability tests are used less often and for slightly different purposes. The child has been started and, it is hoped, has come quite a long way in the development of his tool skills in reading, writing, and arithmetic. Unless there are special reasons for giving it more often, the learning ability test usually is given only once during this three-year period. It is given then to check the conclusions drawn from earlier testing, to call the attention of teachers to changes that might be taking place in the comparative learning skill of individual youngsters, and to aid the teacher in arranging as much individualized instruction as she can manage.

By the time of elementary and junior high school grades, a child is giving clear evidence of his mastery of the tool subjects, or his lack of it. This is the level at which individual differences in school achievement really begin to show dramatically. It is also the level at which decisions are made for and with most students, decisions about the courses their learning should take in the years just ahead.

The performance of the child on a learning ability test will yield some evidence that may be helpful in reaching or recommending a decision about him. How skillful is this student in his use of the principal tools of academic learning, regardless of his marks? By affording children a chance to demonstrate their skill with the tools of learning—in a situation that is completely separated from behavior in class—the learning ability test gives everyone concerned some added and useful insights.

In the high school years, learning ability tests often take on added importance. Increasingly, the scores have the dual purpose of helping the teacher to understand the student better and thus to teach him better, and of helping to guide the student toward the kinds of learning that best suit his abilities and his hopes. For about half of the students in the average high school, this is the time when the question arises: Should I go to college? If so, which one? And this is the time when the learning ability test gets more public attention than it enjoys either before or afterward in the academic world— probably more attention than it deserves—because at this level it comes to be known as the "college admission" test or the "scholarship" test.

These tests answer just one question for student, counselor, parent, and admissions officer: How well can this student use the basic tools of academic learning, in comparison with other students who have succeeded in the academic work of this college? They do not ever tell anyone that he will succeed or fail in college generally or in a particular college—only how well equipped the student is to compete with the other students who will be attending the same college. They help the student and those concerned for him to estimate the odds favoring his success in a given higher institution.

Learning ability tests of approximately the same kinds, reflecting skill in verbal and mathematical symbolism, are used all the way through college and graduate school, into the professions, and finally, into the upper levels of business and professional occupations. At all levels and for all purposes, they have these two characteristics: (1) They ask the student to demonstrate his skill with the tools of learning, and (2) their interpretation is no more and no less than a comparison of the individual's performance on the test job with the performances of other individuals on the same job.

CHAPTER 3

THE WHY AND HOW
OF ACHIEVEMENT TESTS

What are achievement tests? Primarily they are jobs devised to permit the student to demonstrate what he can do with the information, skills, and ideas he is supposed to have learned in school. Achievement tests differ from learning ability tests in this one major respect: Learning ability tests measure intellectual skills that the individual has acquired over a very long period of time and from many sources, such as home and community, as well as school; the achievement test ordinarily measures knowledge and specialized intellectual skills learned over a shorter period of time—a month, a semester, a year or two—and taught directly in school. The learning ability tests measure skill in the use of academic tools, while the achievement tests measure the amount and quality of learning that has taken place in a specific area. In its most general form, the purpose of an achievement test is simple: to find out whether the student has learned what the teacher has been trying to teach him.

There are several critical steps in the building of a good achievement test. The first step is to decide what the student should be able to do as a result of instruction. This is what the technicians, in their strange and wonderful language, call "stating the goals of instruction in terms of behavior," and its importance cannot be emphasized too strongly. It means that since the teaching is intended to change the student in some way, and since whatever change occurs will occur deep in the intricate mechanism of the student's intellect, the best way the teacher can know that the change has been wrought is to deduce it from behavior of the student that can be seen. Thus, a properly stated goal of instruction would be: "Can perform the four fundamental processes with decimal fractions quickly and with 90 per cent accuracy," in preference to "Knows decimals"; or "Writes clear, complete sentences in his written work for other teachers," rather than "Has learned fundamentals of sentence structure." If the objectives are stated only in broad generalizations such as "Understands the tragedies of Shakespeare," then the measures of achievement resulting from that instruction may well be no more than broad generalizations and often will hit wide of the mark.

While it is probably too much to expect that any teacher should at one time write out in behavioral terms all the teaching goals of all his instruction, gradual development of goal statements and constant editing of them will lead toward clearer assessment of student learning. Two useful references are available as sources from which goal statements can be adapted or borrowed: *Elementary School Objectives* and *Goals of General Education in High School,* both published by the Russell Sage Foundation, 505 Park Avenue, New York City.

Some goals of instruction are, of course, much harder to describe and evaluate than others. Teachers whose instructional objectives lie in this intangible category, which involves such aspects as insight, understanding, and appreciation, find it easier to describe what they are doing by first writing down the goals in their general outline, and then for each goal stating what "symptoms of learning" they would look for in the behavior of the students. The excerpt here is from a teacher's statement of goals in a high school senior unit on *Macbeth*. These goals are of the intangible kind: enjoyment and interest.

Goals	*Symptoms of Learning*
If the unit of instruction on Shakespeare's *Macbeth* is successful, most students will:	Behavioral evidence which the teacher will accept as a sign that the student is growing toward the stated objectives.
I. Enjoy *Macbeth*	
A. As a dramatic experience	A. Shows some evidence of emotional reaction to hearing or reading *Macbeth*.

B. As a revelation of Elizabethan thought

B. Asks questions or contributes comments or seeks additional information on the place of Elizabethan thought in Anglo-American history.

C. As a link with the heritage of English-speaking people

C. Asks questions or contributes comments or seeks additional information on the character of life in Elizabethan England.

D. As a sample of popular drama

D. Quotes favorite passages voluntarily, seeks and enjoys a part in a dramatization, does personal research on some aspect of the play or on Elizabethan character, volunteers opinions, debates points of interpretation, disagrees with the teacher or class, shows special sympathy for a particular character, mimics or burlesques some character, etc.

II. Have an increased interest in reading and seeing more drama

Reads part or all of some other Shakespearean drama, reads part or all of some modern drama, watches all of a Shakespearean drama on television, mentions opportunities to see or hear serious drama, inquires about such opportunities, comments on dramas he has already seen, brings to class old playbills and other artifacts of the drama, suggests dramatizations or other class activities, asks the teacher for more class work in drama, etc.

The point of goal-stating would not be so long belabored if it were not that everything that follows in the making, using, and interpreting of achievement tests hangs on this point. Somebody has to state specifically what is to be learned in terms of what the student will be able to do, before a reasonable measure of learning achievement can be built.

The teacher, having organized his materials and methods of instruction, then proceeds to teach in the way he thinks will help the student toward the kinds of learning that are his objectives. But eventually he must find out whether the student has learned the things he sought to teach him. He knows that he would get an unreliable answer if he asked the pupil to tell what and how much he has learned, because the pupil usually does not know precisely what he has learned until he is given some chance to try it out. The teacher could shadow the pupil for months after the instruction, noting his every move to see whether his behavior in class and elsewhere gives evidence of the desired learning; but this is hardly practical. So he devises a set of tasks for the student that will give him a chance to demonstrate, on the spot, the nature of his learning.

If the teacher's goal for the pupil has been simply the recall of information, the test-building is easy: Ask him questions, written or oral, that require him to recall the desired information. If the goal is some academic skill, such as translating certain passages from a foreign language, the test is still easy to build: Give the student some passages to translate. By and large, however, looking at the list of things he set out to teach, the teacher is interested in a variety of approaches, requiring several kinds of tasks:

1. Several tasks that require the student to recall the most important pieces of the specific information he was expected to commit to memory

2. Several tasks that require the student to generalize and draw conclusions—both from information he has remembered and from information provided

3. Several tasks which require the student to apply newly learned generalizations to new and unfamiliar information

4. Some tasks which require the student to discover and reveal relationships between newly learned information and information previously learned

This teacher has now outlined the bases for an achievement test for his student, in that this set of jobs permits the student to demonstrate positively the amount and quality of his learning. Two important aspects of the test are that (1) there are test tasks for every one of the four important teaching goals and (2) every one of them requires the student to do something. Note the active verbs: recall, generalize, apply, and discover. These are essential characteristics of a good achievement test.

If the goal is a subtle or complex one, such as the ability to suspend judgment while gathering evidence for the resolution of an issue, test-making becomes very difficult indeed. The task presented by such a test would have to contain a situation in which the student has opportunities to express or withhold judgment during the time he is collecting information—a very complicated procedure to put into a test. In fact, the testing of complex goals is so difficult, and so little amenable to paper-and-pencil techniques, that some teachers close their eyes to it altogether.

But people who put effort and thought into it do build tasks that call for demonstration of complex and insightful learning. Some of them are tasks that cover several days, in and out of the classroom, during which the teacher observes, records, and interprets student behavior. Others are tasks that can be presented in written or printed form and given to a whole group of students at one time, such as these:

Suppose you walk into a science classroom and find the following piece of equipment on the desk:

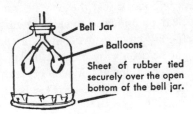

Bell Jar

Balloons

Sheet of rubber tied securely over the open bottom of the bell jar.

4. You properly conclude that the class is studying:
    (A) How does a vacuum pump work?
    (B) How is breathing aided by the diaphragm?
    (C) How does the heart pump blood through the body?
    (D) What is the composition of the atmosphere?

5. When this equipment is used, the balloons will be inflated. Which of the following procedures would inflate them and keep them inflated for a few minutes?

   (A) Move the sheet of rubber in and out of the bell jar as rapidly as possible.
   (B) Move the sheet in and out of the bell jar one or two times a minute.
   (C) Push the sheet up into the jar and hold it there.
   (D) Pull the sheet down below the jar and hold it there.

Skill in making test questions that require the student to demonstrate complex learning must be learned the hard way, by effort and practice and professional instruction and critical study. This is the key skill for those who would prepare good test questions. There are hopeful signs that formal instruction in test-making will have a place in the undergraduate training of all teachers before another generation passes. When that happens, there will be fewer teachers who strive for learning outcomes like literary appreciation and then assess progress with what amounts to a literary vocabulary test.

The next step is to study the test, finding out how well it works, after it has been used for the first time with a group of students. This is done in many ways, but usually is aimed at answering two questions: (1) How well does the test work as a whole? (2) How well does each question or task in the test work? These two kinds of study are called "test analysis" and "item analysis," respectively. They are necessary for the construction of a good achievement test. Until he has tried out a test task in a "live" situation, the test-maker cannot be sure that the task will work just the way he wants it to work. The directions may be clear to him, but unclear or misleading to the student. The task itself may have grown out of a special point of view or a particular insight held only by the test-maker, but to the student who has a slightly different insight it will be ambiguous. In a good achievement test, the intent of the test-maker is crystal-clear in every task; the student does not have to wonder, "Now, what is he getting at here?" Perhaps the test-maker, with his more advanced knowledge of the subject, may make many test questions too difficult for the less sophisticated learner. The characteristics of the "raw" or untried achievement test are the results of human fallibilities and can be avoided or corrected only through the tryout processes of test analysis and item analysis.

This step of studying the test may best be illustrated by a test-maker (let us call him the examiner) who has made a final examination for his course in American history and plans to administer it to three sections or classes numbering 100 students all together. He has 100 questions in the examination, about half of them requiring straight factual recall and the other 50 attempting to get at more complex kinds of learning, such as insight and ability to generalize. He gives the test to his hundred students, scores them by giving one point for each correct answer, and then turns to the business of finding out how well his test worked. The first thing he does is to make a graph of the scores earned by all his students. Figure 2 shows what it looks like. The graph surprises and disappoints the examiner a little. The average score is in the low sixties. He had thought it would be higher, and he certainly had expected his half-dozen best students to turn in perfect or near-perfect papers. The scores below 40 look bad, too. (This examiner does not know it now, but if he pursues his interest in testing over the study of many tests, he will discover that this distribution of scores is a good one, especially for a raw test. The fact that no one earned a perfect score and no one got a zero score is evidence that the test is difficult enough for the better students and easy enough for the poor ones—indeed, an average score of about 60 per cent correct responses is what the professional test-makers try for.) He decides that an analysis of responses to each test question would be worth the drudgery it involves.

Instead of merely counting up the number of correct responses given by the total group to each question, the examiner sets out to compare the students in the top quarter on the test with the students in the bottom quarter in their responses to each question. As the criterion for designating students in the "top" and "bottom" quarters he uses the total score on this same test; the necessary assumption is that he has more confidence in the capacity of the total set of questions to discriminate between learners and nonlearners than he has in the capacity of any one question to do this. The result, for ten of the questions, is shown in Figure 3. When he begins his study of this question analysis, the examiner feels he is approaching answers to

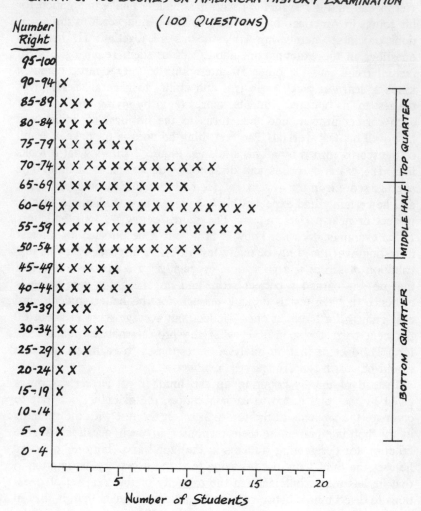

FIGURE 2

GRAPH OF 100 SCORES ON AMERICAN HISTORY EXAMINATION
(100 QUESTIONS)

FIGURE 3

NUMBER OF CORRECT RESPONSES TO EACH QUESTION
BY HIGH GROUP AND LOW GROUP

Question No.	High Group (25)		Low Group (25)		Difference	Comment
	No.	%	No.	%		
46	24	96	8	32	+16	OK
47	16	64	14	56	+2	?
48	19	76	4	16	+15	OK
49	1	4	4	16	−3	? Difficult
50	15	60	1	4	+14	OK
51	23	92	21	84	+2	? Too easy
52	14	56	5	20	+9	OK
53	2	8	11	44	−9	?
54	1	4	0	0	+1	? Difficult
55	9	36	2	8	+7	OK, but difficult

his puzzle. On Question 46, a straight recall-of-information question, all but one of his high group gave the correct answer but only eight of the low group answered correctly; this tells him that the question discriminated between good students and poor students and thus was "working" for him in the test, the principal purpose of which was to discover which students were learning well and which were not. On Question 47, almost equal numbers of highs and lows gave the correct answer—meaning that the question was not working well for him in discriminating between good and poor students; it might have other virtues, such as reminding all students that this is an important piece of information to remember, but with this group it is not a particularly good test question. Question 48 seems to be working, but Question 49 looks very peculiar. It obviously is too difficult the way it has been presented, but what is there about it that leads more of the poor students to give the correct answer than the good students? Something misleading in the way it is written? A closer look at the wrong answers given by the good students might supply a clue to what is wrong with this one, so it is noted for future study. Question 53 is another that seems to be working in reverse—more of the poor students answered it correctly than did the good students; look at the answers on this one, too. Question 54 is altogether too difficult in this form, probably one of the questions that kept the best students from approaching a perfect score. And so on—through all 100 questions.

When he has completed his analysis of the 100 questions, the examiner concludes that he has about 50 that are of appropriate difficulty and discriminate pretty well between good and poor students; they can be used again, just as they are. He has another 20 that are too easy or too hard, or do not discriminate well, but they do not work in reverse and he may want to use them again just to include the topics they cover. Some editing might improve them, too. This leaves him with 30 questions that did not work well in this test and will need some careful work before they are used again.

This long illustration provides a rough picture of the procedures in a test tryout. Professional test-makers use somewhat more refined statistical techniques and are concerned also with still other characteristics of tests and questions, but the methods of test analysis and item analysis are approximately the same as those of the examiner here. Three references will be of particular use to the teacher who is undertaking analysis of his tests for the first time: *Shortcut Statistics for Teacher-made Tests,* and *ETS Builds a Test*—both available from the Evaluation and Advisory Service of Educational Testing Service, Princeton, New Jersey—and a filmstrip work kit, entitled *Making Your Own Tests,* available from the Cooperative Test Division of ETS.

The final step in building an achievement test is one that teachers find practically impossible to accomplish with the tests they make themselves. This is the process of testing large numbers of students so that there can be reference groups with which to compare an individual's score and give it meaning. It is the process called "norming" in the technical language of testing. The need for it grows out of the fact that on most achievement tests no one realistically can say that a good student should earn such-and-such a score. How could the examiner in the illustration of the third step say, with any justice or reason, that to pass his course students would have to answer correctly 70 of his 100 questions? Three-fourths of his students earned scores below 70. If he clung to a notion that "70 per cent is passing," a too-popular bit of nonsense in our folklore, he would have to conclude either that the class was unusually dull or that he was a poor teacher. Our examiner properly regarded his test as a sample of student performance that itself merits study and improvement—and also properly assigned values to the test scores on the basis of comparison of each student's score with the scores earned by all other students.

Because of the practical difficulties that stand in the way of the teacher who seeks to obtain norms on his test outside his own class, almost all teacher-made tests are limited in their interpretation to class norms. Some large city school systems develop city norms for certain tests that are used system-wide, and occasionally there are comparative data on the test performances of students in a state-wide group. It is important to note, however, that almost without exception the tests that are used for comparisons that go beyond the teacher's own classroom are standardized tests. The balance of this section on how tests are built, therefore, pertains almost wholly to the standardized tests.

Comparison data, test performance information about a lot of other but similar students, are especially important when the performance of a particular student or class is to be interpreted. (The word "norms" is being de-emphasized by many testing people who care about how test information is used, because too many teachers have built the word into their vocabularies with a wrong connotation; in this erroneous view, "below the norm" means the same as "subnormal" and has all sorts of emotional consequences that are both inaccurate and unfortunate. Instead, test people prefer to talk about where a student "stands in a comparison group.")

To provide the comparison data needed for score interpretation, professional test-makers administer the final form of a test to large numbers of students whose performance reasonably could be expected to throw some light on the meaning of one individual's performance. Thus, if a test is designed to measure achievement in American history at the tenth-grade level, the publisher will have it given to many tenth-grade students in a number of different schools and will make a "distribution" of their scores like the graph made by the examiner in our illustration. Then, when the test is given later to another child in the tenth grade, it will be possible to see how his performance (score) compares with the performances of all those other tenth-graders. He may do better than 99 per cent of those other students, or worse than 99 per cent of them, or somewhere in between, but his score has a comparative meaning that is useful.

This simple procedure, hidden though it often is by elaborate statistics, is the essence of norms or comparison data in interpreting test scores. The publishers of standardized tests go to a great deal of trouble and expense to provide useful comparative data for interpretation of scores on their tests, although, in general, the most immediately useful comparison data are those collected by the teachers in their own schools.

In a school system that uses standardized tests well, there may be available to the teacher the following kinds of comparative data for, say, the above-mentioned tenth-grade achievement test in American history:

1. Distribution (a graphic tabulation as in Figure 2) of scores earned by all the students in the individual's own class

2. Distribution of scores earned by all the students in all the American history classes in the individual's school

3. Distribution of scores earned by tenth-grade students in all American history classes in the local school system, city or county

4. Distribution of scores earned by all tenth-grade American history students in the state (this is a rare occurrence)

5. Distribution of scores earned by tenth-grade students in American history in a nationwide sample of schools—this distribution provided by the publisher

These five kinds of comparative data have been arranged here in their likely order of usefulness and meaning in the interpretation of an individual student's performance on the achievement test mentioned. Comparison with class data has the most meaning because it shows how well the individual has done his test job in comparison with other students who have had the same teacher, textbooks, and curriculum. Comparison with school data shows the student in relation to others who have had the same curriculum and books but different teachers. Comparison with system data lines him up in a still larger but somewhat more heterogeneous group. The comparison becomes more difficult to interpret as the group with which the student is compared grows larger and less homogeneous. The so-called national norms are the least useful of all because one so seldom knows just what kinds of students are in the comparison groups.

If the teacher has these five kinds of comparison data available for the American history test, then student A's test performance very well can have five different comparative meanings:

	Class	School	System	State	Publisher's
Score	Norms	Norms	Norms	Norms	Norms
142	48%	44%	56%	60%	65%

These interpretations would mean that student A was slightly below the middle of his class on the test, somewhat farther below the average of all classes in his school, but above the average in his state and better than 65 per cent of the students who took the test in the publisher's sample. These various interpretations tell the teacher and the student how his performance stacks up in comparison with several kinds of "competition."

It is important to note that even with a standardized test the most useful kinds of comparison data are the kinds that the local school must itself build. The publisher starts a test off with the best kinds of interpretations he can obtain, but teachers and schools have to invest still more time and effort to provide for a test the interpretations that have the most meaning. This can be done only through a systematic collection and statistical treatment of scores earned by students in the class, in the school, and in the school system.

The most widely used score type among achievement tests is the percentile rank, which simply reports the proportion of students in the comparison group who have been surpassed by the student who earned this score. A score with a percentile rank of 67, for example, means that the student who earned it did better on the test job than 67 out of 100 students in the comparison group. This makes it important to know what kinds of students were included in the comparison group.

Although percentile rank scores are convenient and explicit, they have one weakness: The difference in degree of achievement between, say, a student who is at the ninety-fifth percentile rank and one who is at the ninetieth is not the same as the difference in achievement between the student at the fifty-fifth percentile rank and another at the fiftieth. Since in any large group many students tend to be near the average on a test, the difference between fifty-fifth percentile and fiftieth percentile rank may be only one point on the test, while the difference between the ninety-fifth and ninetieth percentile ranks may be six or seven points on the test. This trickiness of interpretation, which grows out of the fact that percentile rank simply represents the individual's position among a ranked group of students, usually results in an overinterpretation of differences in the middle of the score scale and an underinterpretation of differences at the extremes of the scale.

To get around this difficulty, "standard scores" are frequently used. With standard scores, the intervals at different points on the scale are equivalent in terms of the number of correct answers they represent on the test. On the College Board score scale, for example, the person who is "average" in the quite select group taking the Board's examinations earns a score of 500. In general, the Board scores range from 200 to 800. The difference between scores of 450 and 550 is almost exactly the same as the difference between 650 and 750.

There are many variants of the standard score; so no one set of numbers will identify it. One variant of the standard score that is gaining popularity in school use is the "stanine" score, based on a scale which breaks the total range of performance on a test into nine segments; the score of an individual is one of the numbers from one to nine and it shows which of the nine categories of achievement his performance falls into when compared with the performances of other students like him.

A third type of score used with some achievement tests—almost wholly in the elementary grades—is the grade-equivalent score. This had great popularity and wide use thirty years ago, but its popularity is waning. It, too, is a comparison score. Its scale is established by finding the average scores of children in two successive school grades and dividing the difference between the two grade averages by ten; thus, if the average raw score on a reading test at the beginning of the sixth grade is 27 and the average at the beginning of the seventh grade is 35, the score of 27 has a grade equivalent of 6.0 and the score of 35 a grade equivalent of 7.0—with the raw score points between the two averages expressed by means of decimals such as 6.1 or 6.9.

The statistics of this kind of interpretation probably are as respectable as those used in computing percentile rank, but the grade-equivalent score is capable of misleading interpretations. For example, a boy in the middle of the sixth grade takes an arithmetic achievement test and earns a grade-equivalent score of 8.7. His parents, and too often the teacher, are tempted to conclude that the boy is a high eighth-grader in arithmetic. He is, of course, nothing of the sort. He is a good sixth-grade student who did somewhat better on that arithmetic test than the average eighth-grader. If that boy were post-haste promoted to the middle of the eighth grade in arithmetic (thank goodness this seldom happens), he probably would be lacking other skills learned in the seventh grade and might fall miserably on his face. This is the unreasonable kind of interpretation that is all too easy with a grade equivalent score.

Another dangerous kind of interpretation is also too easy. Suppose a boy in the sixth grade takes a reading test and earns a grade placement score of 4.1. This does not mean that he is a "fourth-grader in reading," an all too natural interpretation; it means only that his performance on a test was the same as the average performance on that test by fourth-graders in the publisher's sample of children. If he were taken literally to be a "fourth-grader in reading" and given fourth-grade books to read, instead of books suited to his maturity level in content but less difficult in language, it would be quite possible so to turn him against reading that he would be years overcoming the handicap. Such shortcomings as these have led most testing specialists to prefer to use certain other comparative scores rather than the grade-equivalent score.

There is one further principle that applies to interpretation of all achievement test scores. The score is an estimate, certain to have some error in it because the test takes only a sample of all the things that one might ask the student to do to demonstrate his learning. And it must be treated as such. One should not pretend to read distances in millimeters with a yardstick that comes free with a can of paint. Neither should one pretend to read precise meaning out of a test score that is only an estimate. Fortunately, the major publishers of standardized achievement tests now are providing with more of their new instruments a score system in which the score of an individual student is a band or an interval, rather than a precise score point. The example below is taken from the examiner's instructions for interpreting scores on the *Sequential Tests of Educational Progress,* a widely used series of achievement measures.

How to compare a student's performance on any two tests taken:

1. If the shaded areas for any two tests overlap, it is impossible to say with any certainty that the student's standing on one test is higher than his standing on the other test.

2. If the shaded areas for any two tests do *not* overlap, one can say with considerable certainty that standing represented by the area farther to the right is higher than standing represented by the area farther to the left.

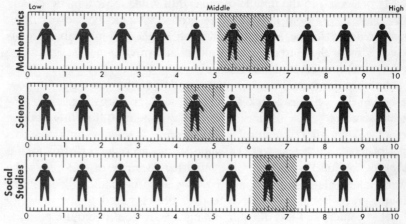

The shaded areas for Mathematics and Social Studies overlap; there is no important difference in standings on these two tests. The same is true of Mathematics and Science. However, the shaded areas for Science and Social Studies do not overlap. The student is higher in Social Studies than in Science ability, as measured by these tests.

The "band" score shown for Mathematics extends from the fifty-first percentile rank to the sixty-third and means that if this student took the test over again many times his score would fall within this band two times out of three—an enforced recognition of fact that a test score is an estimate. In general, the longer the test the narrower the band and the more accurate the estimate. The bands shown here are for scores on tests of considerable length (70 minutes—50 problems in mathematics) and represent degrees of test consistency as high as any found in tests practicable for school use; hence, these score "bands" are about as narrow as they can be on any achievement test.

Some achievement tests have scores reported on a punched card, arranged in such a way that the punch or rectangular hole in the report card represents the interval in which the student's score has fallen—an effective way of reporting performance when test papers are processed by machine. And, of course, the stanine score is itself a kind of band score, since there are but nine score values on the whole scale. Other achievement tests have scores reported as single points, but their manuals usually caution the user to surround each score point with a band of described width to avoid overinterpretation of small differences.

Perhaps the most revealing of all the comparisons used in interpreting test scores—and easily the most difficult to interpret—is the comparison between the student's own past and present performances. The degree to which he has changed and grown is the clue to whether he is learning as much and as well as he can. All comparisons and scores are significant only as they serve to appraise the development of the individual.

CHAPTER 4

WHAT MAKES
A TEST GOOD?

One principle comes first in any discussion of what makes a test good: Even the very best test is good only when used for its specific purpose with the kinds of students for whom it was intended. That is, although tests can be and some are universally bad, no test can be universally good, equally appropriate and useful for many purposes and all students. Hence, it is not possible to say of any test just that it is good; it is necessary to say that it is good for a particular purpose with particular students; or, if several tests are being compared as to their usefulness, that this test is better for this purpose with these students than are the other tests.

Excellence in a standardized test is not only specific but comparative. Since no test has yet achieved the ultimate perfection, nor even approached that perfection, it is wiser and more practical to say that this test is better than others for a given purpose and for stated kinds of students (or not as good as other tests), than to say categorically that one test is good and imply that others are poor.

With goodness judged in relation to a purpose and in comparison to other tests, it is possible to go on to the technical characteristics that make a standardized test good. The two most important are:

1. A good test measures what it is intended to measure (it is "valid").
2. A good test yields a dependable score (it is "reliable").

Each of these characteristics is sufficiently complex—sometimes subtle—to warrant extended discussion.

A Good Test Measures What It Is Intended to Measure

Strange as it seems, the question of what a particular test does measure is often not answered by reference to the name of the test, or to what the author says it measures, or even to what it generally looks as if it measures. For instance, in 1961 the principal reference in test-publishing listed twenty-three standardized achievement tests in English for the junior high schools, not including tests in composition or literature—and no two of these tests measure exactly the same kind of learning. One achievement test in "sixth-grade geography" may require recall of many place-names and products, while another test with the same name but a different author will ignore products and stress cultural differences. One test in "first-year physics" will require recall of the classic laws of motion and energy, while another of the same name will call for solution of practical problems.

Every test author tries to measure what he thinks are the most important outcomes of instruction in a subject. No two authors (or committees) have yet come up with exactly the same list of outcomes to be tested. Until there is a single, standard list of teaching objectives to which all schools and teachers subscribe (an altogether unlikely circumstance and probably undesirable), standardized tests will continue to measure different sorts of learning with different kinds of content. And until there is such an unlikely standard list of objectives, schools and teachers will have to choose those among the published tests available which test what they are trying to teach.

There are several aspects to the process of determining the suitability of a specific test in a given situation. The joint efforts of the test-maker and the school or teacher are required if a successful match is to be made.

The authors and publishers of standardized achievement tests owe to the users of each test a specific description of what each question is intended to measure. To be most useful, this description should indicate clearly what the student is expected to do; i.e., punctuate between units in a series with commas, recall in proper sequence the political events leading to World War II, compute the mechanical

FIGURE 4. *Publisher's Analysis of Test Content, Science Achievement Test for Junior High School Grades**

ITEM NUMBER	RIGHT ANSWER	GRADE 7 – % RIGHT (NORMS)	GRADE 8 – % RIGHT (NORMS)	GRADE 9 – % RIGHT (NORMS)	DEFINE PROBLEMS	SUGGEST HYPOTHESES	SELECT PROCEDURES	DRAW CONCLUSIONS	EVALUATE CRITICALLY	REASON QUANTITATIVELY	BIOLOGY	CHEMISTRY	PHYSICS	ASTRONOMY	GEOLOGY	METEOROLOGY	ITEM NUMBER
PART ONE																	**PART ONE**
1	B	64	72	79		•									•		1
2	H	78	86	93		•		•			•				•		2
3	A	54	62	69	•										•		3
4	F	57	65	72	•							•					4
5	A	81	89	96		•							•				5
6	H	50	58	65		•						•					6
7	C	46	54	61		•					•						7
8	E	38	46	53		•					•						8
9	D	79	87	94	•							•					9
10	F	62	70	77		•					•						10
11	D	26	34	41		•					•						11
12	G	21	29	36			•				•						12
13	B	23	31	38					•		•						13
14	G	18	26	33					•					•			14
15	D	67	75	82		•					•						15
16	G	51	59	66	•						•						16
17	B	55	63	70		•							•				17
18	G	52	60	67	•						•						18
19	A	80	88	95		•					•						19
20	H	58	66	73		•							•				20
21	C	61	69	76		•					•						21
22	H	51	59	66		•					•						22
23	D	33	41	48						•			•				23
24	G	43	51	58						•			•				24
25	D	31	39	46	•								•				25
26	F	27	35	42		•							•				26
27	D	41	49	56		•							•				27
28	F	59	67	74		•									•		28
29	B	41	49	56		•									•		29
30	H	33	41	48			•								•		30
PART TWO																	**PART TWO**
1	C	58	66	73				•			•						1
2	H	43	51	58	•						•						2
3	B	59	67	74			•				•						3
4	E	51	59	66				•			•						4
5	A	59	67	74	•								•				5
6	F	37	45	52	•								•				6
7	D	41	49	56			•						•				7
8	F	70	78	85			•						•				8
9	B	65	73	80	•								•				9
10	G	72	80	87		•							•				10
11	D	39	47	54					•	•			•				11
12	F	52	60	67					•	•			•				12
13	B	69	77	84					•	•			•				13
14	H	50	58	65					•	•			•				14
15	A	44	52	59					•	•			•				15
16	H	53	61	68		•							•				16
17	C	25	33	40	•								•				17
18	F	30	38	45		•										•	18
19	C	57	65	72			•						•				19
20	G	66	74	81		•	•					•					20
21	C	35	43	50			•					•					21
22	G	44	52	59		•						•					22
23	B	28	36	43		•						•					23
24	H	52	60	67				•						•			24
25	C	73	81	88					•	•							25
26	G	41	49	56		•						•					26
27	D	81	89	96				•							•		27
28	G	33	41	48		•									•		28
29	B	11	19	26					•						•		29
30	E	21	29	36		•							•				30
NUMBER OF ITEMS IN CATEGORY					4	25	14	4	5	11	21	8	20	5	5	1	

* Reproduced with permission of the publisher from the *Teacher's Guide* for the Cooperative Sequential Tests of Educational Progress, 1959, p. 77.

advantage of a given set of pulleys, recognize the intent of an author by reading his text, subordinate details in preparing an argument. Several of the newer standardized achievement test series do provide such lists of what they attempt to measure and are better tests because of it (see Figure 4 for an example). With lists like these, the teachers or committees responsible for selection of tests can compare the measurement goals of the test directly with their own goals of instruction and judge which test provides the best "fit" with their teaching.

The builders of standardized tests often do a great deal more than just make tests and list their contents. They study what is taught in schools throughout the country. Since there is no common curriculum used by schools everywhere, and because the methods of teaching vary as much as the subject content, even in a "traditional" subject like beginning algebra, the test-maker who hopes to have his instrument used widely tries to concentrate his questions on those topics or skills which are taught by the most teachers and, even more important, by the best teachers. To find out what is taught by the most teachers and the best teachers, even in one subject at one grade level, is a long and difficult job. The test publisher known best by the authors of this book spent nearly three years and enlisted the aid of more than a hundred outstanding teachers in developing the first raw questions for a new achievement test series—just to have some assurance that the new tests would have content related to the goals of good teachers in today's schools.

Whether or not the publisher has provided a content listing for his standardized test, the school people who consider using it have a clear responsibility to study the test, question by question, and judge its fit to their teaching before they undertake its use. This "trying on for fit" process is essential if the school is to avoid the multitude of headaches that grow out of a situation in which pupils truthfully can object: "They teach us one thing but test us on something else."

Trying a test for fit is a careful, detailed process, but it is not immensely difficult if it is done by a committee of teachers and administrators so that the work can be shared. It involves three steps: first, stating in detail what skills and information the school wants to measure; second, discovering in detail exactly what each test measures; third, comparing the two sets of detail to see how well the test and the teaching match. No one outside the school can do the job of stating what the school wants to measure; so the first job is wholly one for the teachers and administrators. The second job—stating the detail of what a test measures—has already been done for some tests by their publishers (as in the example cited in Figure 4); if a content analysis has not been provided by the publisher, the school needs to make its own, using a homemade form arranged like the one shown in Figure 4 and studying the test item by item. The third job—comparison of the two analyses—is relatively easy and permits the committee to see what proportion of the test is really relevant to the things they want to test, and what proportion of items is irrelevant to their needs.

Relevance alone, however, should not be the sole determining factor. Before arriving at a decision, the teachers should examine the item content comparison with two thoughts in mind:

1. To what extent are all important areas of teaching covered by this test? It is wholly possible that a test may do an excellent job of measuring most of the major areas being taught but may completely ignore two or three important areas of instruction. A particular test may still be used in spite of this deficiency, but the teachers should recognize the shortcomings when interpreting the results.

2. Is there a proper balance of areas in the test? Or is too much emphasis being given to certain areas of instruction at the expense of other areas? The relative importance of various topics to be covered in the classroom must be determined. If the test is to reflect adequately what has been taught, the balance of topics in the test must correspond to the balance of topics in the instruction.

When standardized achievement tests are used to estimate how well students are learning the things they are being taught, there is no alternative method for matching tests to teaching. Thus, if teachers and administrators want to assure themselves that the tests they use actually measure what they intend the tests to measure, they have a job to do. The fit of test to teaching obtained by this method is what measurement specialists call "content validity," and it is the single most important thing to know about an achievement test. Without it, achievement testing is scarcely more than random activity and contributes little to the work of the school.

Assessing the fit of a test of ability or intelligence or academic aptitude to the needs of a group of students is both more difficult and more technical than assessing the suitability of an achievement test. In the former case, the content of the test is not usually the same as the content of instruction, but consists of tasks or jobs that resemble the mental tasks involved in school learning and sometimes look strange to teachers. So a detailed analysis of test content by a committee of teachers and administrators is not appropriate in the case of an ability test.

Rather, the analysis of an ability test to discover the extent to which it measures what it purports to measure should be undertaken by members of the school staff with training and experience in psychological measurement. This is not to say that there is anything involved that teachers cannot understand, but merely an acknowledgment that the manuals in which the information is to be found are written in the specialized language of testing. For example, "construct validity" and "predictive validity" are the most important characteristics of ability tests for school use; both depend upon very careful definitions of meaning; and predictive validity is described in terms of statistical data.

The construct validity of an ability test is described by the publisher when he relates why the authors have chosen this particular set of tasks on which to have students demonstrate their learning skills. Assessing the comparative construct validity of two tests, as it bears upon a given situation in which a test is needed, the specialist interprets from the information given in the test manual and infers an advantage for one or the other in the particular situation.

The predictive validity of an ability test is described by the publisher when he reports (in statistical form) the relationship he has found to exist between the scores students earn on this test and their later success in school learning. If the scores generally indicate which students will achieve great success and which will not, the test is said to have comparatively high predictive validity. It is a job for the specialist to study these reported data and to judge which test has not only the highest predictive validity, but which test appears to have proved its predictive validity when used with students like the ones he wants to test. Quite often the specialist will collect data on a new ability test during its first few years of use in his schools—to "check out" the predictive validity of the instrument with his particular school population. This is good practice.

Whether it is an achievement test to be judged as to its fit with instruction by a committee of teachers and administrators or a test of learning ability to be assessed by specialists in terms of its validity for the school's students and testing purpose, the capacity of a standardized test to measure what it is supposed to measure is its most important characteristic.

A Good Test Yields a Dependable Score

No test of intellectual performance yet designed even approaches the level of precision now attainable in the physical measurement of man. In comparison, the measurements used in education remind one of the little girl who told the school nurse, "No, ma'am, my mommy doesn't use a thermometer to tell when I have a fever—she just feels." Even so, some mothers are more accurate feelers than others. It is the same way with tests.

The reliability (dependability) of a good test is built into it by the author and publisher. It is preserved by the wise user who follows directions exactly in giving the test and applies common sense in interpreting the scores. Test-builders develop reliability in their instruments by application of principles that have been known and used for a long time.

1. *The principle of multiple samples.* In order to obtain a reliable estimate of a person's real level of performance one must observe him in that performance more than once—in fact, the more observations of performance that can be taken, the more reliable will be the conclusion based upon them. When we want to know how good a hitter a professional baseball player is, we look at his batting average, which is a summary of his performance at the plate over many times at bat. We describe the skill of golfers and bowlers in terms of their "handicap," which reflects their performance in many rounds or games. The odds on a horse in a race are based on its past performance in all races entered. All of these situations involve multiple samples. The test-builder knows that the teacher who uses his test will obtain a

more reliable estimate of the student's ability or learning if the test asks many questions than if it asks just a few. This is why most standardized tests used in school are so long, have so many questions, and take so much time; the more samples taken of the student's performance, the more reliable the test score.

2. *The principle of standard tasks.* This second source of reliability means that every student who takes a test must be confronted with exactly the same questions, presented in the same way. Since the individual's performance usually has a value only in terms of its comparison with the performances of many other individuals, it is critically important that everyone who takes a test should have exactly the same job to do. This is how the "standardized" test gets its name; its content, arrangement, typography, and directions are "frozen" when the test is normed. The test used to compare one youngster (in geometry, say) with other students all over the country is exactly the same as the test given to those other students in the comparison group. It has to be, if the comparison score is to be reliable.

3. *The principle of standard conditions.* Just as every student who takes a test has the right to be confronted with the same questions as all other students (for the sake of a reliable score), he also has a right to take the test under conditions that are the same as those provided for other students. Obviously, a cramped seat, stuffy air, poor light, or noisy neighbors will affect the test performance of some people. So will an examiner who stumbles in the reading of directions or bustles around the room while the test is being taken. For this reason, the publisher of every good test includes in the test manual a description of standard testing conditions and a strongly worded plea to the school to reproduce these conditions as closely as it can when the test is given. This can be done by almost every school with a little effort.

4. *The principle of standard scoring.* If a test is to have a reliable result, the performance of a student upon it must have the same score value no matter who does the scoring. That is, two different people (or twenty or a hundred) scoring Bill Jones's test accurately must come up with exactly the same score for Bill. The principle of standard scoring is fundamental to the concept of the standardized test; individuals running the same race under identical conditions must be timed by the same watch. An essay test or a "long-answer test"

is much less reliable than a test in which point credits for various answers are clearly established and objectively applied.

The characteristic of reliability in a test comes, then, from four sources:

Multiple samples—more questions, more reliable score
Standard tasks—everybody gets exactly the same questions
Standard conditions—a "fair shake" for everyone taking the test
Standard scoring—scorers give credits consistently and impartially

How much reliability is enough? There are some gross generalizations about reliability that will be almost as useful in the normal interpretation of scores on ability and achievement tests as a great deal of statistical knowledge:

1. In general, a test score should be based on student performance over at least half an hour of testing time to be reliable enough for individual interpretation (40–50 questions are the usual minimums, though there are exceptions).

2. A test composed of "thought questions" or complex problems has to be much longer in time than a test composed of factual recall questions in order to yield a score of equal reliability.

3. The major scores on almost all widely used standardized tests are sufficiently reliable for individual interpretation—but any subscores that are based on as few as 10–15 questions should be taken with a grain of salt.

So much for the amount of reliability a test ought to have in school use, except for two comments on the application of these ideas to the tests that teachers prepare for their own classes. The daily or weekly quizzes that teachers give and record in the grade book are exempt from the described minimum requirements in reliability so long as the teacher does not make any important or final judgment of the student on the basis of any one of those quiz scores; the teacher may form some judgments on the basis of the sum of several quiz scores, and that judgment is likely to be quite reliable because it is based on performance over many questions. On the other hand, the teacher who bases half of the final grade on a three-question essay test may have reason to wonder about the reliability of the judgments he makes.

The characteristic of reliability, usually expressed as a "coefficient of reliability" or a "standard error of measurement" is something a test must have in order not to be a poor test, but having it is no guarantee that the test is a good one. In this respect, test reliability is somewhat like the wheels on an automobile—necessary, but no real indicator of how good the car is. So it is used in limited but important ways in giving meaning to test scores. Test users should take reliability into account by:

1. Shying away from use of very short tests in measurement of important skills or learnings; the tests that are expected to make substantial contributions to important decisions about a student are long ones, calling for many samples of his performance.

2. Attaching very little importance to small differences in scores (such as the difference between an IQ score of 104 and one of 108); the difference has to be fairly large, even on long tests, before it is reliable enough to work with.

3. When short tests are used, such as periodic quizzes, drawing conclusions only from the total score earned on many of them.

4. Remembering that for certain kinds of learning, such as the ability to write an essay, a test necessarily contains a very small sample of the student's performance; such a test may be useful in several ways, but its score is notoriously unreliable.

5. Remembering that even the best tests are only samples of behavior and never making any final decision about any student solely on the basis of one test score.

Good tests are reliable enough to contribute important information about a student to a pool of knowledge about him that is gained from a variety of sources.

Danger Signals

Discussion of the major crimes against effectiveness of tests has been withheld to the end of the chapter and has been limited to a fairly terse listing. These are some of the characteristics of tests and users that keep testing from being as good as it could be:

1. *The too-short test.* With demands on school time so heavy, teachers and administrators sometimes are tempted to choose the

test that requires the least time, especially if some publisher intimates that "this short form is almost as reliable as tests that take twice as long." If a test is to be given at all, in nearly every case it is important to give the best and most dependable one that can be found. One cannot expect to obtain a reliable estimate of learning ability or learning progress in a twenty-minute test, any more than he would expect to obtain a reliable check on a child's physical condition by having him stick out his tongue.

2. *The "wide-range" test.* This is the too-short test in disguise. There are only a few of them around. They are promoted as being suitable measures of ability (or achievement) for people of many ages—from third grade through second year of college, for example. Since only a small part of any such test can be material suitable in difficulty for one individual, the effective part of the test may amount to no more than half a dozen questions—making it a very short test, indeed.

3. *The test selected-from-on-high.* Watch out for the test that has been picked by one person and "imposed" on the school. It may be a very good test in terms of all that its publisher can do, but it can also involve problems. There are good reasons for occasional use of city-wide and even state-wide tests, and on these occasions teachers will get all the good they can out of the externally selected tests. But, for the most part, the greatest benefit for the most students will result through the use of tests that have been chosen by committees of the students' own teachers.

4. *The test with the pinpoint interpretation.* No test measures accurately enough to support a precise, one-point interpretation of a score or a "diagnosis" of small differences between scores. Any test that leads the user to believe he has a precise measurement, then, is subtly dishonest and can lead him into trouble.

5. *The "quick-and-dirty" test.* Good standardized tests are the result of careful and costly work, years of it, which the publisher is only too glad to describe at length. So beware of the test for which there is only a scrawny little folder describing the instrument's background in vague terms. The manual or other material accompanying a good test tells a great deal about it: who made it and why, how the original questions or problems were devised and what they are intended to measure, how and on whom the original tasks were tried

out, what methods were used to test the questions, how many and what kinds of students were tested to obtain norms, how dependable the scores turned out to be with tryout groups, and how precise an interpretation can be made with scores. If detailed information is lacking on any of these points, the test may be a little gem in the rough—but it is more likely to be one of the quick-and-dirties that infest the darker parts of the educational forest.

6. *The test that tells one what to do.* There are no tests like this, but many people think that there are, or behave as if they had taken one. No test yet made, or likely to be made soon, tells anybody what course to take, or that he would be a good engineer, or that she ought to take the airline stewardess training. The most that any test can do is help a student compare himself with certain other kinds of people —in knowledge, in interests, and in related background. The two vocational inventories most widely used in schools, for example, do not tell any student that he should aim toward any particular occupation; they simply tell him how his interests and activity preferences compare with those of successful people in a variety of occupations. As we said, there is no test that tells anyone what to do.

A complete answer to "What Makes a Test Good?" would fill a five-foot shelf. It already has. In this chapter, therefore, only a few highlights have been reflected. Generally speaking, if a test measures what it is intended to measure and does so dependably, and if it is applied and interpreted with common sense by people who know what they are doing, it can be regarded as a good test. And good tests, these days, are not hard to find.

CHAPTER 5

SELECTING
APPROPRIATE TESTS

How Are Achievement Tests Used in Schools?

Like a lot of other tools, achievement tests are used in many ways, only some of them the ways in which their makers intended them to be used. Professional test-makers, observing the variety of uses to which their instruments are put, occasionally are reminded of the scientist whose delicate micrometer was used by his wife to crack nuts. Whether or not such a comparison is apt, the fact remains that in schools generally there are both appropriate and inappropriate uses of standardized tests. When achievement tests fit the goals of learning and measure with acceptable accuracy, they are well used in the following ways:

1. *To assess the development of the individual learner.* This probably is the most important single use of achievement tests in schools. Having estimated the student's ability to learn, and having specified the things he wants to teach him, the teacher from time to time needs to check up on the student's learning progress—so that gaps or lags can be taken care of and so that the instruction may remain appropriate to the learner's needs and attained proficiency. Most of this kind of assessment is done with teacher-made tests, but for measurement of long-term growth or of the more complex kinds of learning, the standardized test usually is employed.

2. *To aid in the academic guidance of students.* At high school and

college level, every student is faced with choices among courses and curriculums. Since the most powerful determinant of an individual's success in any course or field is the success he has achieved in learning similar kinds of things, his grades in related courses and his performance on appropriate standardized tests of learning achievement are effective guides in his planning of the next steps in his education.

3. *To aid in curriculum planning.* Because of the constantly changing world in which young people are being educated, teachers and others in the field periodically review the content and methods of their instruction for the sake of improving them. The goal always is to make the education of every youngster better, more suited to his needs, and better adapted to the environment in which he will live and work. In this constant search for improvement, tests of all kinds play a useful part. Do students learning by method *B* learn more or more quickly than students learning by method *A*? Has our change in the social studies curriculum increased the learning of our pupils? Can we teach as well with large classes and closed circuit television? These questions and many more like them are answered in part every day with the data obtained in the administration of appropriate achievement tests.

4. *To aid in decisions on promotion and admission.* The higher a student climbs on the academic ladder, the more frequently his promotion from level to level will depend in part upon his performance on a test or tests of achievement. Almost always, the tests used for promotion purposes are instruments built by teachers, though at some critical points some schools use scores on standardized tests. But at the point of transition from high school to college, or from junior college to senior college, standardized achievement tests are used quite commonly to provide additional evidence from objective sources and affect institutional decisions to admit students for higher studies.

5. *To aid in school assessment.* It will be wise at once to point out and emphasize the word "aid" in this heading. Too many people, particularly those who are critical of a school or system, or who for some reason wish to denounce public education, seek to prove that one school has a lower average score—or a higher one—than some other school on "a standardized school achievement test." Standardized tests cannot be used alone to judge schools, for even a whole

battery of them will not measure all kinds of learning students achieve. The effectiveness of a school or school system depends upon so many things—community culture, "climate" for education, parent aspirations, citizen involvement, to name a few—that average student performance on standardized tests usually reflects the nature of the community as well as the nature of the school, and in unknown proportions. Nevertheless, professional educators and school board members who are sufficiently interested to conduct inquiries that include or control such factors usually find that standardized achievement tests do contribute in a worthwhile way to evaluation.

Unless they are used actively in one or more of these ways—really used to the extent that both students and teachers recognize their benefits—standardized achievement tests become "busy work" in the schools and might better not be given at all.

How Standardized Achievement Tests Differ from Teacher-made Tests

Even though good standardized tests usually have been built with great care and attention to a number of important criteria, it does not necessarily follow that standardized tests should be substituted for teacher-made tests. When a teacher has the interest and time and training to do it, he can build an achievement test for his students that may well be better for his purpose than any published test. This is true simply because the teacher knows better than anyone exactly what he is trying to teach those students and can fit the test to the teaching. But since a teacher rarely has the time for the long procedures outlined in Chapter 3, even if he does have the interest and the training, it might be more accurate to say that the very best achievement tests can be built by a school system (city or county or state) using the combined brain power of a committee of teachers to state the goals of learning, some trained specialists to work with the teachers in creating the test content, some statistical technicians to handle and organize the data, and a central office unit to accomplish the endless chores of typing, mimeographing, sorting, and scoring.

Because relatively few school systems can afford the staff and equipment required to conduct this kind of test-building operation, however, there are test publishers—both commercial and nonprofit—who spread the costs across many schools by doing this work in a central place and selling the finished products to the schools. There are notable differences between the teacher-made tests used in most schools and the standardized tests used by the same schools. Some of the more important ones are listed here:

1. If the teacher is competent in test-making, his homemade test probably will have a better "fit" with his teaching goals than any standardized test. He can tailor his test exactly to his course and his students, while the publisher of a standardized test in the same subject must build his test in accordance with goals and expectations that are common among many teachers in many schools. However, if the teacher is not experienced and skilled in test-making, he may build such a poor or inappropriate instrument that it has far less fit with what he is teaching than the test made by the distant publisher.

2. The teacher-made test can be constructed to cover much smaller units of time and instruction than is economically feasible for a publisher to build. That is, publishers ordinarily cannot build a test for "the third six-week period of tenth-grade instruction in American literature," because only a few schools teach the same course in the same way at the same time and the market for such a test is therefore small.

3. The teacher-made test usually can be scored and reported back to the student more quickly than a standardized test; this is not necessarily so, but it is the way things work out in most schools.

4. On the other hand, the standardized test usually is more comprehensive in its coverage than the teacher-made test. While the teacher-made instrument may follow the instruction with better fit, the instruction itself runs the risk of being limited by the goals of the teacher or of omitting or de-emphasizing learnings that are generally accepted as desirable.

5. The standardized test usually has been built by people who have had training and experience in the technical work of creating test jobs that require students to demonstrate complex learnings. That is, many tests built by teachers tend to depend on recall of information, while the best tests done by professionals go beyond recall and measure also such things as insight, ability to generalize, skill

in application of knowledge to new situations, and other desired learnings.

6. The standardized test usually has been tried out, pretested, before its final form is used. Few teachers have had the time or the training to do this—or the necessary access to many tryout schools. As a consequence, standardized tests generally are more efficient measuring instruments than most teacher-made tests.

7. Finally, the standardized test offers comparison data or norms with which the school can make some interpretations of individual performance the very first time a test is used. The publisher's norms are listed as the least useful of all possible comparison data for a test, but they do give some meanings to test scores that are not attainable with locally constructed tests.

These listed differences between standardized tests and "homemade" tests have led to school practices in testing which are sensible and practical. For tests that cover short units of instruction, weekly and monthly quizzes, semester examinations, tests in unique courses or experimental classes, and longer units of instruction that involve content or methods different from general practice, most schools depend on testing instruments made by the school staff. For tests that cover longer periods of learning, a year or two, and tests that attempt to measure the more complex learnings, most schools depend on standardized tests. So a school in which testing is done most effectively is certain to employ a combination of homemade and standardized tests in such a way that the two kinds of instruments complement each other when the school uses them to understand and guide the learning processes of students.

How Schools Select Standardized Tests

It is no easier to generalize about schools than about persons, since every one is different from all others in almost every respect; but there are some practices that many schools follow and that appear to have enough merit to make them desirable for all schools. One such practice is that for the selection of standardized achievement tests. Whether in a single school or in an administrative unit of schools, such as a city or county, the schools that get the most out of the standardized achievement tests they buy select them in approximately this way:

1. The school develops a written statement of the kinds of learning it wants to test. This statement is made up of the goals of teaching mentioned earlier and usually contains as many as possible of the learning goals that are important in the curriculum, especially those difficult to measure with teacher-made tests.

2. Reference sources are studied in order to obtain as long a list of test possibilities as can be made, and reviews and professional critiques are studied. Half a dozen or so of the most promising tests are selected for further study on the basis of the preliminary search.

3. "Specimen sets" of the half-dozen tests are purchased from the publishers, containing all descriptions and manuals as well as single copies of the tests themselves.

4. Committees of teachers and supervisors then compare each of them with the list of learning goals they want to measure, question by question. The result is a complete and detailed analysis of the degree to which each of the tests fits the pattern of learnings the school wants to measure. This procedure amounts to a "trying on for size" of each test considered.

5. The publisher's manual for each test should explain who prepared the original tasks or questions, how the tryout was done and how well the tasks appear to have worked, how dependable the scores have been in other uses, what kinds of students were included in the comparison samples that support the tests' norms, and practical aspects, such as how much time the test requires and how much it costs.

6. It is likely that several of the tests being considered have been built with care and that they cost about the same in both time and money. Among the tests that are appropriate in these practical characteristics, the school chooses the test that has the best fit with what the school wants to measure—as determined in the "trying on for size" described in step 4 above. It is more sensible to choose a test that goes beyond the specifications than one that falls short of them.

Whether the test-selection process is described in four steps or forty, there are two aspects of it that are essential: (1) knowing exactly what is to be measured and writing it down in detail, and (2) examining the tests themselves, item by item, to judge how they fit.

How Do Standardized Achievement Tests Differ from Each Other?

Standardized achievement tests differ, one from another, in two equally important respects: They differ in what they measure, and they differ in how well they measure.

The how-well-it-measures characteristic has been described in Chapter 4 in some detail. In general, a good achievement test measures well enough for school use with individuals when it is long enough to yield a reliable score, when it has been tried out and edited and revised to a point at which all its questions have demonstrated that they work, and when the publisher has given the test for comparison data to reasonably large groups which he describes carefully. These are technical characteristics which the school man learns only by study of the test-makers' manuals and a review of the research reported by other users. Since the sale of test materials is a fairly big business in American education, there is an element of competition in test publishing and the school representative has to be able to distinguish between advertising claims and honest-to-goodness supporting data.

There are some real "clinkers" among tests advertised for sale, particularly among achievement tests in academic subject matter—tests that look "official" because they are printed rather well, but have no supporting data other than vague claims by the author and no background information to provide interpretation. Then there are tests offered for sale by a fringe group of individuals and companies whose principal product is workbooks or records folders or office supplies and whose tests are sidelines. Generally speaking, one is more likely to find tests that measure well listed in the catalogues of the major test publishers; for it is in these major agencies that one finds the resources and staff to do professional work in test-building.

The difference among achievement tests in what they measure is almost infinite. Since the goals of teaching in some subjects—social studies, for example—are themselves almost without number, it is natural that the tests devised to assess achievement of these goals should represent a wide diversity of content. Without attempting to exhaust the possibilities (it would take the rest of the book), it might be worthwhile here to illustrate some of the different kinds of test content that appear in good tests of English achievement at the high school level.

1. Which word is misspelled?
   (1) outragous   (4) surprise
   (2) medieval   (5) none wrong
   (3) query

2. Select the word which best completes the following sentence. My worst fears were _____; he had forgotten the tickets for the game.
   (1) ratified   (4) corroborated
   (2) validated   (5) fortified
   (3) confirmed

3. Which of the following books is the most humorous?
   (1) *The House of Seven Gables*   (3) *Treasure Island*
   (2) *Tom Sawyer*   (4) *Silas Marner*

4. Choose the one name that does not belong with the other three.
   (1) Thomas Hardy   (3) Thomas Wolfe
   (2) John Galsworthy   (4) Arnold Bennett

5. Choose the characteristic which the three similar names in Item 4 have in common.
   (1) American dramatists (3) English novelists
   (2) American novelists   (4) English critics

6. The lecturer indicated that he would begin (   ).
   (1) with the third man, Socrates, first
   (2) with the third man, which is Socrates
   (3) with the third man first, known as Socrates
   (4) with the third man, Socrates

Mark Twain's habit of swearing was revolting to his wife, who tried her best to cure him of it. One day he cut himself while shaving and recited his entire vocabulary. When he finished, his wife repeated every word he had said. Mark Twain looked at her calmly and said, "You have the words, dear, but you lack the tune."

7. "Entire vocabulary" means all the
   (1) profanity there is.
   (2) profanity that Mark Twain thought suitable for his wife to hear.
   (3) profanity that Mark Twain knew.
   (4) words that Mark Twain knew.

8. Mark Twain's comment meant that
   (1) he wanted his wife to try again.
   (2) his wife's performance had made a deep impression on him.
   (3) his wife's performance lacked emphasis and conviction.
   (4) his wife had no ear for music.

9. Where would you go to find commentaries or observations on a familiar theme such as wealth?
   (1) *Webster's Unabridged Dictionary*
   (2) *Encyclopaedia Britannica*
   (3) *Bartlett's Familiar Quotations*
   (4) *Readers' Guide to Periodical Literature*

According to the standard reference list of published tests, Oscar Buros' *Mental Measurements Yearbook,* there are more than a hundred published tests in the field of English. It is safe to say that no two of them measure exactly the same knowledge or skill. Because achievement tests differ one from another so much, the school must analyze carefully the content of tests it is considering for use. Saying that "Bill earned a score above average on a standardized English test" is scarcely more descriptive than just saying "Bill is above average." The questions remain: "Above average in what?" and "compared with whom?" Achievement tests are quite specific, and they must be regarded that way.

A Good Test Is Practical for School Use

A test that is "good" for school use has been molded in many ways to suit it to the cold facts of life in schools. The practicality of any test is, or should be, the last criterion applied in the selection of a standardized test by a particular school unit, but it is an important criterion, for if a test has serious practical shortcomings in a given school, its usefulness may be lost completely. The point can be made here by a simple listing of some of the factors of practicality that help to make a test good.

1. *Low cost*. Because school business practices change slowly, most schools have to buy test materials out of a small special budget account rather than out of larger funds earmarked for "textbooks" or "instructional supplies." Very often the expenditure of fifteen to twenty cents per student for testing in any one year will wipe out this special budget. Low cost, then, within the reach of school officials with limited budgets, is a practical characteristic of a good test.

2. *Convenient time units*. A school day is made up of many different activities, interlocked in a time schedule in such a way that rearrangement of the schedule for one group or class is likely to cause a disruption of the schedule for many others. The schedule is built of class periods ranging from thirty-five minutes to fifty-five minutes in length. A test that requires sixty minutes to administer in one session, therefore, would be inconvenient to use in most schools. So tests that take longer than forty minutes to administer (and many of the good ones do) are arranged in parts or subtests that can be finished in one class period.

3. *Ease of administration*. Since group testing in most schools is done by the teachers and the counselor (if there is one), the test materials and directions need to be arranged in such a way that they do not require a squadron of accountants to keep track of them and a platoon of lawyers to translate them. The simplest of the achievement tests in the upper grades have a test booklet and an answer sheet for each pupil, plus a booklet of directions for the examiner and a record sheet or two. This is enough for any examiner to manage in a testing session, which is a little tense anyway. The need of a stop watch for close timing, or special pencils for marking, or answer sheets with little buttons to be picked off, or long and complicated directions to be read to the students every few minutes adds to the difficulty of administering the instrument. Ease of administration means that the student can demonstrate his knowledge or ability with a minimum of gadgetry and interruption, according to concise directions that both he and the examiner understand.

4. *Ease of scoring*. The work of the school in testing is only one-

third done when the test has been given; scoring and interpretation remain. And the scoring of any test in quantity is a drudgery. Use of teacher time for this counting job can hardly be justified (unless the test requires judgment in the scoring, in which case the teacher or a trained aid has to do it); therefore, the scoring operation is arranged whenever possible so that it can be done by clerks or, better yet, by machines. From the school's point of view, it does not matter much how a test is scored, so long as the scoring is accurate, fast, and inexpensive. No two tests are likely to be scored in the same way, however, or with equal ease and economy, so scoring characteristics often affect a school's choice of a testing instrument.

5. *Ease and clarity of interpretation.* After a test has been scored, someone has to translate each score into a form that has useful meaning to the student, to his teacher, and to his counselor and parents. No one gains much by learning that Mary's score on the science test was 75 (75 what?) or "in the sixth stanine," or "a percentile rank of 87," or "a grade-placement of 10.3," or "a standard score of 63." Mary's score has to be translated into some meaningful comparison: How well did she do compared with the others in her class? How well compared with others of her grade in the publisher's norming group? How well compared with her teacher's expectations of her? How well compared with her own expectations? Within the limits of the reliability of the scores, how do her test scores compare from subject to subject? How does this test performance compare with her last test performance? Do the test results point to any particular strengths or weaknesses? Do they contribute to an indication of a trend or change in her pattern of learning? These are interpretations of a test score and the only really useful outcomes of testing. Test performance has to answer these questions and others like them to be worth the effort and money that testing costs. A good standardized test will provide all of the materials and most of the information needed to make these interpretations relatively easy to accomplish.

6. *Client acceptance.* This final form of practicality is not easy to give an accurate short name to, so "client acceptance" will have to do. It means that the teachers look at the test as a reasonably good measure of at least some of the important things they have been teaching. It means also that the students who take it regard the test as a reasonable collection of tasks on which to demonstrate their learning or

their ability. And it means that parents can see the test as a reasonable means for demonstrating and checking their youngsters' learning progress. To aid in parent acceptance, a few publishers have prepared materials especially to be sent home with students after an important testing, explaining the school's uses of the test information and providing general interpretations of the individual student's scores. The sharing of test score information with students and their parents is standard practice in most testing; a good test should have instructions or materials to make it easy for the school to do it.

Are Objective Achievement Tests Better than Essay Tests?

This question has no single answer. Whether one type of test is better than the other for a particular use depends upon several things: the kinds of ability or learning to be measured, the purpose of the measurement, how the scores are to be used, who makes the test, and who interprets the scores.

When one wants to obtain an idea of how well another person can write—how well he organizes his ideas in writing, his facility in expressing subtle nuances of meaning, his ability to establish and exploit mood, his adroitness with the "narrative hook," his skill in the subordination of arguments to essential points, and so on—one asks him to *write* something, preferably a long piece of writing. This is an essay test. Its advantage over the objective test in this instance grows out of the definition of a test established in early chapters: A test is a job. As a work-sample of the student's present ability to write essays, then, nothing is better than an essay test.

But the essay test is not a wholly accurate and reliable measure, even of the ability to write an essay, for two reasons: (1) The writing of one essay is but a single sample of this ability, a sample that often is affected by the topic assigned, the pressure of writing in a testing situation, the lack of references, and other circumstances that affect the writing quality of even the best writers from day to day; and (2) the grading of the essay test sample is partly a subjective process in which several different examiners, equally competent, will ascribe different values to the writing sample because the perception of a written passage, like perception of personality, varies from person to person and from day to day within a single person. For these reasons that affect the accuracy and consistency of its scores, an essay test is a notoriously poor *predictor* of future learning success—even of success in essay writing.

The main trouble with the essay test is that so many people try to use it for the measurement of other things than the present skill of the student in writing essays. When the history professor assigns a "paper" on the political issues of the Reformation and posts grades on the assignment, he *thinks* he is grading the knowledge, insight, and synthesis of students in history, but what he is really grading, in a large but unknown measure, is their essay-writing ability. Even so, for that professor the essay test or assignment may work better, as an evaluative device, than any objective test he might give—if he has had no training or experience in the building of objective tests and is prone to limit his test to questions of factual recall. For the assessment of complex learnings, a long and carefully graded essay test *can* be better than a poorly constructed and probably limited objective test. Better to bail with a small teacup than with a large sieve.

If (and *only* if) the following conditions are present, an essay test may provide a more useful measurement than an objective test:

1. The teacher is either strongly prejudiced against all objective tests or does not know how to prepare good objective test questions.

2. The teacher wants to assess the progress of his own pupils in learnings that involve insight, synthesis, or analysis and organization of subject matter concepts (learnings that require more advanced skill in the preparation of objective test questions).

3. The teacher will write down his criteria for grading ahead of time and observe them strictly.

4. The teacher will grade all of the essay examination papers himself.

5. The examination time permits a long essay.

6. The student's grade on one essay is not regarded as an accurate measure of his skill.

However, even the teacher who meets all six criteria with ease will do well to keep in mind the weaknesses of essay examinations that usually are overlooked: Teachers who rely on essay tests often are careless in preparation of the questions or topics to be discussed, leading students into quandaries of interpretation even before they can begin to write; they often fail to provide directions telling the student how exhaustively to treat the topic; finally, they tend to grade the essays on the basis of criteria that have not been revealed explicitly to the student. All of these weaknesses in the run-of-the-mill essay test tend to reward the verbally facile student who has devoted effort to finding out "what the teacher wants"—which is not always what the teacher thinks he is testing.

It is obvious to those who have investigated essay testing that there is as much need for professional instruction in the preparation and grading of essay examinations as there is for training in the preparation of objective tests. Examples of the best modern practices in essay testing may be found in the *Handbooks* for the essay tests of the *Sequential Tests of Educational Progress,* published by the Cooperative Test Division of Educational Testing Service, Princeton, New Jersey.

As for objective tests, it must be said that it is easier to build poor ones than good ones. To build an objective test that measures more than the ability to recall tiny fragments of factual knowledge requires training and technical skill. Its main shortcoming, like that of the essay test, lies in the fact that so many teachers make objective tests in the belief that they are measuring a broad set of learnings when their tests actually are measuring only a small part of those learnings.

For many purposes of classroom testing, the written essay is to be preferred over objective tests because precise measurement is not of the utmost importance in any one test and because the teacher often is as interested in the value of the essay-writing experience for the student as in the measurement aspects of the exercise. On the other hand, when the score a student earns on a particular test is likely to have some importance for his instruction or guidance—or if it is to be used in making decisions about him—a carefully built objective test will measure his learning far more extensively and accurately.

The hard answer to the question with which the section opened boils down to this: Given two examiners fully trained in the arts of achievement testing, one building essay examinations and the other objective tests, the examiner with the essay tests probably can do a better job of estimating a student's present skill in creative writing, but the examiner who builds objective tests can provide more valid and reliable estimates of just about every other kind of school achievement. And the objective test is always more successful than the essay type when it comes to predicting academic success of any kind. Are objective achievement tests better than essay tests? As we said, it depends on what you want to test and who builds the tests.

How Much Testing Is TOO Much?

The question posed in the section heading can be answered both generally and specifically. The general answer first: Any testing that is not used immediately and importantly to improve the understanding and instruction or guidance of students is too much testing. There is too much testing in a school that gives only one standardized test a year if that one test is not wrung dry of its information about the learning of students and the information put to work.

On the other hand, in a school where testing is an integral part of teaching and the results of testing are constantly fed back to students so they can watch themselves grow and shore up their weak spots—in such a school, some testing can be done every day of the year and not be too much.

Testing frequently is discussed as if it were something separate from instruction, with no educational value itself. The taking of a test—a good test that requires the student to demonstrate the important things he has been learning—often is as instructive for him as a similar period spent in other classroom activities. Hence, it is more pertinent to ask how closely related is the test to the learning goals for students, and how well its results are used, than to inquire how much time it takes.

No school faculty becomes expert in testing and the utilization of test results overnight. If a faculty or its leaders feel that more and better uses can be made of modern testing techniques, it is wise first to make a modest start with the addition of one new assessment procedure—be it a standardized test or an in-service training program on teacher-made tests—study its application carefully and extract every bit of usefulness from it, then to think about adding a second test or procedure.

Change at times should be in the other direction, too. In some schools certain tests have been used for a long time out of habit. The test results are given a cursory look before they are filed in cumulative folders, teachers give little heed to students' test performance in the conduct of their instruction, students do not know exactly why they take this examination, and nearly everyone has forgotten why this test was adopted in the first place. Such a test is ripe for pruning; teachers, counselors, and principal should ask themselves some pointed questions about "getting their money's worth" out of the test and, if no one comes up with some convincing reasons for retaining it, the test should be quietly dropped. The same principle applies to everything we do in education or business: If a practice or procedure no longer produces the results for which it was originally adopted, discontinue it.

Testing in schools is intended to improve the instruction and guidance of students. Any testing that does not contribute substantially to the quality of instruction or guidance is too much testing.

CHAPTER 6

TESTS AS TOOLS
IN TEACHING

Every good teacher knows that learning is something done by individuals, not by groups. He knows, too, that each individual student is different from every other individual student in the class—in what he will learn, in the rate at which he will learn, in the kinds of stimuli to which he will respond, in how he will go about learning, in the levels his learning will reach, and in the satisfactions that learning will give him. Thus, though the teacher with twenty-seven pupils for practical reasons cannot use twenty-seven different methods and texts and assignments, he knows that this would be the best way to go about his job. Fortunately for teachers, most of the students in a group probably will respond to instruction planned for the typical student; so most of them will learn what the teacher is attempting to teach—and only a minority will need to have stimulus or method or content tailored to them as individuals.

But the teacher needs constantly to find out whether the approach he is using really *works* with most of the students, whether his method is one that leads the students to learn, whether the content and practice material he has laid out are appropriate, whether the results of his instruction are what he had hoped for. If he does not find out these things as he goes along, his instruction is quite likely in time to "miss" a majority in the class—in which case he is not a good teacher. Furthermore, he needs to find out which students are the few for whom his instruction is substantially inappropriate—and what kinds of difficulties they are having. In other words, the good teacher tries to prove for himself that his students are learning what he wants them to learn as he and they go through the teaching-learning process. It is this continuing audit of individual educational growth which is the main use of tests in teaching.

The particular uses of tests in teaching fall into six fairly distinguishable categories: Tests are used to judge capacity to learn, to guide teaching, to check learning progress, to discover learning difficulties, to improve teaching techniques, and to assess teaching effectiveness.

Judging the Capacity of Students to Learn

Whether his goal is to help six-year-olds to read or to help graduate students to formulate an hypothesis, the teacher gains in confidence when he has some assurance that each student probably can learn the things he has to teach. It is for the sake of both teacher and student that instruction at all levels of schooling is almost always preceded by some effort to judge the student's capacity for learning from that instruction.

It has been demonstrated time and again that human learning is a cumulative, continuous process. One's ability to learn skill X is determined largely by the progress one has already made in learning skills U, V, and W. What the pupil brings to the learning of a new task really is not an abstract thing called "intellect" but a whole collection of experiences and earlier learnings which he can relate to the new task—plus a desire to learn, called "motivation." And, of course, the formal instruction contained in the long process of school education is arranged in a sequence from elementary to complex, from easy to difficult, from obvious to subtle. We are not always sure of the exact sequence of experiences necessary in the learning of certain things— witness the half-century-old hassle over the relative priorities of phonics and whole-word attack in the learning of reading—and we realize that the desirable sequences often differ among different learners; but generally people agree that learning is a sequential growth in which the human being assembles an ever-larger collection of learnings which have pertinence to the new things he has to learn and which he can bring to bear on them.

Judging the capacity of a student to learn something new involves a procedure that is deceptively simple in theory and equally complex in execution. The simple theory is that if you want to know whether Jill can learn to extract square roots you just find out how many of the things that lead up to learning square roots Jill has already learned. If she has learned all of them fairly well, and if in addition she is not unwilling to try learning square roots, then chances are very good that she can be taught how to extract square roots. However, if she is lacking several important learnings that lead up to square roots—a couple of bad holes in her long-division skill, for example—she has little chance of learning square roots successfully. Finally, the theory concludes, if all the prerequisite learnings have been acquired, the student has the capacity to take the next step in learning with success; if he has not acquired all the prerequisite learnings, then he can go on only after the missing ones have been filled in.

There are great differences among people in the intellectual powers with which they are endowed by heredity. But it has not yet been possible, in measurement, to separate these powers clearly from those with which people have been endowed by their environments. It has been observed that people who probably are more generously endowed by nature than the average learn new things at a faster rate, and that they appear to require a shorter exposure to experience in order to assimilate it into their learning equipment than do others, but it is still clear that even for the very bright, learning is the process of applying skills obtained in past experiences to new problems. When we say that we measure "capacity to learn," what we are really trying to measure is the likely speed with which the student will learn a new subject or skill and the depth and complexity of learning he is likely to achieve. The question becomes: "Will this student be able to assemble and apply his related experiences quickly enough to accomplish the desired new learning in the period of time allowed for it?" Students who take three times as long as other students to learn a new skill, whether the reason be hereditary or environmental in origin, are said to lack capacity to learn it for purposes of the normal class. As a consequence, the practical definition of capacity to learn, the definition always used in school measurement, includes hereditary as well as environmental factors without attempting to distinguish between them.

But How Are Tests Used to Make These Judgments? And Why?

Teachers in the primary grades give tests to estimate the readiness of young pupils to begin formal instruction in reading. If a child's previous experience somehow has trained him to pay attention to small differences in small things—can he, for example, note quickly that one kernel of corn in a row is facing in a different direction from all the others?—he is more likely to be able to distinguish "*b*'s" from "*d*'s" in printed words than a child whose perception tells him only that here are a lot of little things that look alike. If the first child can demonstrate his skill in a number of perceptions like this and certain other skills involved in reading readiness, his learning probably has reached a level at which he can learn to read with little trouble. But the child whose previous experience has not equipped him quickly to see small symbolic differences would have an extremely bad time if he were put down beside the first child and forced to compete in reading. So the second child is set to work on the kinds of things that will give him experience in seeing small differences, and his reading instruction is postponed for the weeks or months it takes him to develop the prerequisite skill.

Thus, with tests, the primary teacher makes her judgments about the capacities of pupils to undertake the formal instruction she has to give.

In the middle grades, a fourth-grade teacher (for example) has not only tests but a whole lot of additional information to help her in estimating the capacity of her new pupils to learn the skills designated for that year. She has the record of the marks each student has earned in the first three grades, some notes passed along by earlier teachers, and, often, the opportunity to talk with the earlier teachers about the learning characteristics of those students who have been in the school before. By this time, each student has a record of learning performance that is highly useful in estimating his capacity.

The record of learning performance is somewhat untrustworthy, however, because it is hard to determine whether a D in arithmetic means that Billy learned very little in arithmetic or that he was inattentive in class—or whether a B means that Sally learned a lot or that she turned in her homework neatly and on time. Pupils, like teachers, are human beings, too, with reactions to teachers and school that do not always reflect accurately what they are learning and how much. Furthermore, pupils change as they mature, and they sometimes "outgrow" the characteristics that dominate their records of past performance. All these things add up to enough weaknesses in the record of learning performance to make periodic uses of tests worthwhile, as a source of insight into learning progress from a slightly different angle.

The teacher may find that there is sufficient spread between the best readers and the poorest readers in the class to warrant setting up several different levels of instruction and content in reading, and on the basis of individual records and test scores she knows pretty well which students should be assigned to each group. She keeps group membership flexible, knowing that her best judgment will turn out to be wrong in some cases and that some of the pupils will gain on the others or fall back in the course of a semester.

Again, though she may have hoped not to "group" her pupils for instruction in arithmetic, their performances on the arithmetic achievement test indicate that only about half of them are ready to go on with the arithmetic of the fourth-grade curriculum, while the other half are going to need at least a month of review before they go ahead. Should she start the "ready" children off in a group of their own—or hold them up with some other activity until the others are ready, too? This is her problem.

Using tests and other information to judge each child's capacity to learn what she has to teach, then, the teacher does her best to place each one at the point that is next in sequence for him—neither so far ahead of him that a gap exists between her instruction and his previous learning, nor so far behind him that his interest is lost through needless repetition.

At the level of the junior high school, where students begin to have different teachers for some different subjects, tests usually are administered again to help in judging capacity to learn. The process is the same as it was earlier, only now there are several teachers involved and possibly even some choices in courses. If there are two or more teachers in arithmetic, one may take a "fast" group and another the "average" and "slow." If this is the level at which an introductory course in a foreign language is offered for "those students most able to benefit from it," a test of ability in the mechanics and effectiveness of expression in English is likely to be used to help identify those whose previous learnings have led them closest to being ready for a second language. Children with the best command of a first language are likely to be the most successful in study of a second one. At this level some students are highly enough skilled to be able to skip long review periods that are necessary for the average student, such as the traditional eighth-grade program in arithmetic, where the fundamental operations are reviewed and "nailed down" (hopefully) for the last time. In many schools, able students can go on into elementary algebra in the eighth grade, thereby allowing time for more mathematics or for other courses outside the mathematics requirements. In all of these instances—and there are others—performance on a test helps to indicate the student's capacity to undertake a next level, or a more difficult kind, of learning.

At the level of the senior high school, there are more choices for the student—and more hurdles. Some courses and some curriculums require more of certain academic skills at the outset than do others. If a student in the ninth or tenth grade is still having trouble with the fundamental operations of arithmetic, he is not encouraged to enter the algebra-to-calculus sequence. If he shows far better than average skill on tests in English mechanics, he may be encouraged to undertake courses that stress creative writing rather than grammar. If a special course has been set up for advanced work in history, students are asked to demonstrate that their learning has reached a point at which they can undertake the more mature studies. In every case, tests and other evidence are considered together in an attempt to judge the capacity of the individual student to learn the specific things that are to be taught. And in every case this capacity is defined as a level of previous learning in those skills and that knowledge which constitute prerequisites for the new learning. The tests used in schools never support a conclusion that a student cannot learn what is to be taught in a particular course—nor do they help much in deciding whether he will learn it—but they do help to discover whether a student has acquired the prior skills that he must have in order to make that learning efficient now.

Testing as a Guide to Planning of Instruction

The ways of using tests to guide instructional planning are clearly related to the uses described for judging the capacity of students to learn. The teacher's material and methods of teaching are more easily adjusted to the capacity of the students than the other way around. When one can expect students to learn only what their previous learning has equipped them to learn, the teacher has but two moral choices in preparing their instruction: to teach them at a level and in a way in which they can learn—or not to teach them at all. To teach at them when the desired learning is beyond their reach is so wasteful as to be immoral. Schools and colleges attempt to avoid such waste in a variety of ways, many involving the use of tests.

Every school and almost every teacher uses a test at some point in the process of planning instruction that will fit the student and his capacities. Sometimes, the test is an instrument that the teacher has made himself and that he administers to a class of students after they start the course; in this case, he is prepared to make certain adjustments on the spot, immediately. In other cases, the school goes to considerable pains to test students extensively in the spring of the year and to share results with teachers before school is out, so that plans for appropriate adjustment of teaching can be developed over the summer. Whether it is formal or informal, school-scheduled or teacher-managed, testing to obtain evidence for the planning of teaching is an established habit in many good schools. And always its purpose is that of finding out where the student is in his learning development, so that teaching may be planned that will pick him up there.

Testing as a Guide in the Elementary Grades

In the elementary schools, testing to guide instructional planning has been refined to an even greater degree than in the high schools, for the elementary teachers have been doing it longer. And since the elementary teacher sees her 25 to 30 pupils all day every day for a year, she has some advantages (as well as disadvantages) when her job is compared with that of the high school teacher, who sees each of her 150 students one hour a day. The principal advantage of the elementary teacher is her ability to concentrate on her 30 youngsters and to get to know them. A good teacher in a good elementary school starts the process of "getting to know them" several months before the pupils show up in her classroom. She is interested in each of them because her job is more nearly centered on the student than on the subject matter and students are her business, by choice as well as by definition. The fact that Billy has a history of very high test scores and mediocre grades catches her attention and causes her to make a reminder note to ask this year's teacher about Billy; at first look, Billy appears to be the kind of boy who needs to be stretched and challenged and lured into the kinds of more demanding study that satisfy the able mind. Her suspicion is that Billy finds the regular class assignments so easy that they are dull and he does not bother to do them. But what is Pamela like? Her record shows low test scores in everything but spelling—and high grades in everything except "social participation." Donald will bear some early investigation, too, with what appears to be a disability in reading that affects his learning in nearly all other areas. These kinds of things the teacher finds out from tests that have been given in the past to students she has not yet seen, but before she sees them she has begun the process of planning her teaching to fit them and their needs.

When school opens in the fall, since this is one of the grades at which the periodic achievement testing program provides for administration of an achievement test battery, the teacher greets her new class with nearly a week of testing—which she does with great care and with specific provision for the fact that most children like to take tests if they are prepared for test-taking in a sensible way. She volunteers to grade the tests of her class herself, rather than have them sent away for mechanical scoring, for three reasons: (1) She will have the scores sooner, and she wants them as soon as possible; (2) doing the scoring herself, she will have a better "feel" for the kinds of tasks on which the class as a whole does well and on which poorly; and (3) she can observe as she goes along the individual performances of children that may be symptoms of something she will want to investigate further. (Not many teachers want to undertake the drudging task of scoring standardized tests—not even this teacher does it very often—but in this instance she thinks that the small insights that might come from her own scoring by hand will be worthwhile.)

She not only scores the test papers, but goes back to make a "class analysis" of errors after the scoring is done. When it is finished she has what she wants—an objective analysis of strengths and weaknesses of the class in the skills covered by the tests. Her first analysis looks like Figure 5, in which she has tallied the number of students

FIGURE 5

CLASS ANALYSIS OF ITEMS MISSED
on Sequential Tests of Educational Progress

Item No.	STEP WRITING	STEP MATH.	STEP SCIENCE	STEP SOC. STUD.	STEP LISTENING
1	□ ///	////	□ //	Ж //	////
2	Ж	□ /	////	Ж Ж //	Ж /
3	□ //	□ ///	□ ///	Ж Ж /	□ ///
4	////	□ //	Ж ////	□ ///	□ //
5	Ж ///	Ж	Ж	□ //	Ж Ж //
6	////	Ж Ж /	□ //	Ж	Ж /
7	□ //	Ж	Ж Ж /	Ж	Ж Ж //
8	Ж	Ж /	Ж /	////	Ж Ж Ж
9	□ ///	Ж	////	Ж Ж //	Ж /
10	Ж Ж //	□ //	Ж //	Ж	////
11	Ж /	////	□ ///	□ ///	□ //
12	////	Ж //	Ж Ж Ж //	Ж ///	Ж ////
13	Ж //	□ ///	Ж Ж Ж ///	Ж //	Ж /
14	Ж Ж ////	Ж	Ж Ж //	Ж //	Ж
15	Ж ///	□ /	Ж Ж ////	□ ///	□ //
16	Ж	Ж ///	□ //	Ж //	Ж ///
17	Ж Ж	□ ///	////	////	Ж Ж ///
18	Ж ///	Ж	Ж /	Ж	Ж /
19	Ж	Ж /	Ж ////	Ж Ж Ж Ж //	Ж ///
20	□ ///	////	////	Ж Ж //	Ж Ж Ж //
21	Ж Ж Ж ///	////	Ж Ж Ж ///	Ж //	□ ///
22	Ж /	Ж Ж Ж ///	Ж	Ж Ж ////	□ //
23	Ж ///	□ //	Ж	Ж //	Ж ////
24	Ж //	Ж	Ж //	Ж //	□ //
25	Ж Ж /	////	////	////	Ж /
26	Ж //	////	////	Ж //	Ж ///
27	Ж Ж ///	Ж Ж /	Ж Ж ///	Ж //	Ж Ж ////
28	Ж Ж //	□ ///	Ж //	Ж	Ж //
29	Ж Ж /	□ //	Ж //	Ж //	Ж //
30	Ж Ж Ж /	Ж ///	Ж Ж Ж //	Ж	Ж /
31	Ж //	Ж	Ж //	Ж Ж //	////
32	Ж Ж //	□ ///	Ж //	Ж	□ ///
33	Ж /	Ж /	Ж /	Ж //	□ //
34	□ ///	Ж Ж	□ ///	Ж /	Ж //
35	Ж ////	Ж /	□ //	□ ///	Ж Ж //
36	////	////	Ж //	Ж Ж ///	////
37	□ //	Ж Ж //	Ж Ж ////	Ж ///	Ж /
38	Ж /	Ж	Ж	Ж /	////

FIGURE 6

ANALYSIS OF QUESTIONS MISSED
BY 30% OR MORE OF PUPILS — WRITING TEST

ITEM NO.	SKILL	TYPE OF MATERIAL
10	Conventions	Minutes of a Meeting
14	Organization, conventions	Personal Narrative
21	Organization, conventions	Story
25	Appropriateness	Report
27	Organization	Announcement
29	Conventions	Letter
30	"	"
31	"	"
32	"	"

ANALYSIS OF QUESTIONS ANSWERED CORRECTLY
BY 90% OR MORE OF THE PUPILS

ITEM NO.	SKILL	TYPE OF MATERIAL
1	Effective expression	Essay, speech
3	Appropriate expression	" "
7	Critical thinking	Personal narrative
9	Effective expression	Story
20	" "	Personal narrative
34	Appropriate expression	Announcement
37	Effective expression	Personal narrative

who have given incorrect answers for each test item or question. When her tally has been completed, she goes back over the sheet and circles the tally marks for every question missed by ten or more youngsters —a third or more of her class. She draws a little square by every question answered correctly by 90 per cent or more of the class.

Having thus defined and identified the questions in five achievement tests that are both hard and easy for her new class, the teacher examines the test materials to scc which kinds of things are the difficult ones and which kinds apparently have been learned by most of the class. For these particular tests, the publisher has provided an analysis of test content; so the job is easier than if she had to study the test questions themselves; but at the end of her analysis she looks at the questions anyway in order to have direct knowledge of the kinds of test jobs the youngsters are doing easily and the kinds with which they are having difficulty.

Based on reference to the publisher's information on test content, her second analysis sheet (for the test of writing skill) looks like Figure 6. This is the analysis that will directly affect the planning of her teaching, for she finds that most of the questions missed by a third or more of her new class have to do with the conventions of letter writing, reports, and minutes. These are the matters of style, arrangement, forms of address, salutations, and so on in letters, on which these youngsters apparently had not yet been instructed. Her regularly planned unit contained instruction on these things, but she will give that phase special attention when she gets to it, in order to close this gap. The questions answered correctly by 90 per cent or more of the class are revealing, too. Almost all of them are questions of usage, the choice of effective words and expressions in a variety of applications. In matters of language usage, then, this class as a whole probably has achieved a higher level of skill than most others of their age. The teacher is thankful that she will not have to spend extra time in usage drill.

This teacher regards these results of her test analysis as clues to the learning needs of the class rather than as precise "diagnoses," for she knows that the test asks only a half-dozen questions in each learning area. But even clues are valuable.

The same technique is applied to all of the other four achievement tests, uncovering those learnings in which the class as a whole probably needs extra emphasis in instruction—and those on which they need only refresher practice. Knowing so much about the learning accomplishment of her class by the first week of the school year, the teacher can plan her schedule and instruction most effectively. With this early information, she need not teach "blind." She has gained teaching time by not wasting it.

Not all teachers use tests in this way to plan teaching. Some of them do not know about it; others are reluctant to spend the time it takes to analyze performance on long tests. A teacher does not necessarily have to give and analyze pretests to be a good teacher, but this practice—however it is done—helps a good teacher to teach what students most need.

Testing to Check the Progress of Learning

Good teachers not only know what they want to teach to their students, and how they intend to teach it, but they also know how to check from time to time to see whether they actually are teaching it. These are the teachers who are unwilling to accept the notion that exposure to an opportunity to learn is the equivalent of learning itself. These are the teachers who think they have not taught unless the student has learned. They are to be distinguished from another type of teacher, who arranges the content of his teaching in a logical, orderly way, exposes students to it and provides opportunities for practice, then considers the job done; if the student does not learn, it is his fault—not the teacher's.

Tests are used by both kinds of teachers to assess the progress of learning. The difference is that the better teacher uses these tests to assess and revise and improve the teaching as it goes along, while the other kind uses tests only to evaluate, and assign marks to, the student.

There are a couple of prime requisites of testing to check the progress of learning, requisites which even the most experienced teacher cannot afford to ignore:

1. The student must be tested on the goal-skill or knowledge before the teaching is begun, as well as after it has been completed. How can learning progress be assessed if one does not know how much the student knew or could do at the outset? Progress from where?

2. The tests used for this purpose must provide for student demonstration of the goal-skills or knowledge. If the test measures something else, however admirable, or if it mixes in a lot of other things with the goal-skills, the picture it affords of learning progress will be murky indeed.

The first of these requisites is clear enough on its face to need little further explanation. To know whether you have succeeded in teaching something, you need to know how much of it the student already had when you started. Many schools and a respectable number of colleges test for this purpose routinely at the opening of every school year.

The second stated requisite harks back to the section which says that a good test measures what it is supposed to measure. It is the lack of this requisite that can render a test useless, whether it is a teacher-made test built awry or a standardized test wrongly applied. For example: teacher X is teaching toward the goals of understanding and appreciating the poetry of Emerson and Longfellow. Classwork emphasizes analysis and discussion of several poems by each author. Homework assignments include the reading of several more poems and the committing of at least twenty lines to memory. After two weeks, the teacher gives a quiz in which the student is asked to:

1. Scan a new verse, marking its meter
2. Identify the poems from which eight quoted lines come
3. State in one sentence each the meanings of four poems which have been discussed in class
4. Write out the twenty lines committed to memory—forty for an A

None of these test tasks gives the student a chance to demonstrate that he is making progress toward the stated goals of instruction, which were to understand and to appreciate. If the teacher rests content with this kind of learning check, he is in the odd position of teaching in one direction and testing in another. He never does know whether he is producing the kinds of learning he says he seeks. The chances are good that he is not producing the stated kinds of learning; furthermore, because students almost always accept what the teacher tests as being what he wants the students to learn—so in this case, instead of learning to understand and appreciate the poetry, they learn to mark off its meter, to remember which lines belong with which poems, and to remember what the teacher says the poems mean. The lines committed to memory cannot be recalled one week after the quiz. The test has not only missed its objective but has led learning down unknown and unsought paths. A standardized test applied in the same haphazard way, measuring learnings that may or may not be related to the specific goals of teaching, is just as bad.

Let's look in on teacher *Y*, who is also teaching toward the goals of understanding and appreciating the poetry of Emerson and Longfellow. Both content and method are different from those used by teacher *X*, for in this class the study and discussion center around the poets as men in a given social setting with their own particular reactions to it. The question most often raised is: "Why did the poet say it this way?" Homework assignments ask the student to read other poems by the same authors—students' choice—and to figure out what the poet was trying to say, and why. Students are encouraged to read aloud in class passages which they think are especially effective expressions in furthering the poet's purpose. After two weeks, the teacher gives a quiz in which the student is asked to:

1. Read, and describe the author's purpose in, two poems which he has not read before
2. Quote and interpret lines which to him are especially effective
3. Quote and criticize lines which to him are not effective
4. Compare the two named poems in literary qualities
5. Compare the two poems in affective consequence to the reader
6. Compare (as in 2 through 5) one poem by Emerson and one poem by Oliver Wendell Holmes
7. Compare (as in 2 through 5) one poem of Longfellow's and one poem of Robert Frost's
8. Write out any lines from either author that the student may have committed to memory because they appealed to him

These test tasks, while not by any means exhausting the possibilities, give the student a chance to demonstrate how well he is coming along in developing understanding and appreciation of the poetry under consideration. In addition to the evidence provided by the quiz, the teacher keeps an informal record of questions asked in class, volunteered reading of other poetry, and disagreements with the poet's points of view—as evidence of students' personal involvement in the experience.

The important difference between teacher X and teacher Y is this: Teacher Y is concerned with student ability to sense and react to certain ideas as they are expressed by two different poets, and with student interest in seeking further experiences of the same kind. Teacher X, on the other hand—even though he professes the same goals—is satisfied if the students recall certain specific details long enough to feed them back on a quiz. Even if teacher X really were concerned with the same student learnings as teacher Y, he would be likely to produce recall types of learning, rather than reaction learnings, if he used measures of learning which stress recall. With his quiz and other observations, teacher Y has a fairly accurate picture of the effect of his instruction on each student at the end of two weeks; he is in a position to judge whether to go on to still other kinds of learning or to stay with this unit a while longer, until more members of the class give evidence of appreciation and understanding. Teacher X has no evidence on the kinds of learning he has sought to produce; so he must proceed or back up with his instruction on the basis of hunch alone. (The chances are good that he will go on to the next unit, whatever it is, because he has "covered" Emerson and Longfellow.)

In testing to check the progress of learning, then, the teacher needs to make sure that the test tasks are concerned with what has happened to the student—that they require him to demonstrate exactly those skills or kinds of knowledge that are the goals of teaching— rather than with his ability to "play back" the details of the teaching. In order to do this, the teacher must be absolutely specific about two things: (1) what he wants the student to do that he did not do before, and (2) what the teacher will accept as evidence that the student really is learning to do those things.

Finally, the most accurate assessments of learning progress are accomplished when the student is tested with the second part of the "before and after" measurement—taking the same test he took before instruction began, or an equivalent form of the "before" test— after he has had instruction and opportunity to learn. Whether the learning has taken only a short time or has covered a long period, it is the change that occurs in the student that may be fairly described

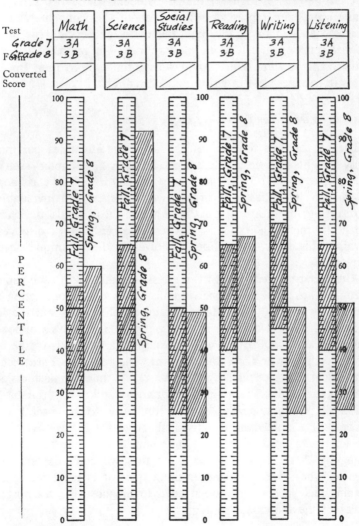

STEP STUDENT PROFILE

SEQUENTIAL TESTS OF EDUCATIONAL PROGRESS

as learning progress. How different is his test performance after the instruction than it was before? The difference, if it is positive, is learning. Figure 7 illustrates the learning progress made by a student between the beginning of the seventh grade and the end of the eighth grade in the kinds of learning measured by the *Sequential Tests of Educational Progress.*

It can be seen in Figure 7 that the student whose two sets of percentile scores are represented stayed about the same in relation to other students in his grade over the two-year period—his learning progress moving along at an average rate—in mathematics, social studies, and reading. He learned substantially more than his classmates in science—less in writing and listening.

Testing to Discover Learning Difficulties

The use of tests to discover the learning difficulties common to many students in a class is described earlier in this chapter—see especially Figures 5 and 6. This technique usually is called "class analysis of learning difficulties" and provides the teacher with invaluable aid in directing his group instruction toward those kinds of learnings which the most students need. When one sets out to discover the learning difficulties of individuals, however, the technique needs to be modified.

A test that has only two or three tasks pertaining to each aspect of learning, such as the ability to handle zeros when subtracting large numbers, is perfectly good for reaching conclusions about the learning difficulties of a class. It will support a class analysis of learning difficulties very well. But it will not support a diagnosis of the learning difficulties of an individual student. The reason is both technical and logical. The technician will say: "Less than ten test tasks [on handling zeros in subtracting] will not give a sufficiently reliable indication of an individual's learning difficulty to be useful to the teacher." The nontechnical individual senses the logic: "With only a few test tasks on a given skill, the chances of doing them right or wrong by sheer chance are so great that we can't depend on the diagnosis they give." Whichever point of view is preferred, the fact remains that special tests are needed to diagnose the learning difficulties of the individual student.

And calling a test "diagnostic" does not make it so. It is unfortunate that a few publishers of standardized achievement tests insert the word "diagnostic" in the titles of instruments that are gross measures of achievement and thus encourage teachers to believe they can accomplish individual diagnosis of learning strengths and weaknesses with these tests. These publishers defend themselves against the criticisms of professionals by pointing to cautions set forth in small print in their manuals, but they have led many teachers to make inaccurate "diagnoses" with instruments not suited for the purpose.

Schools use tests for diagnosis of learning difficulty of the individual in the following way. Periodic tests and other observations indicate that student A cannot read as well as one might reasonably expect him to. Allowing for errors in measurement and the effects of his home environment and the fact that he missed half a year of schooling because of illness, he still appears to have less reading skill than he should. Discovery and repair of his difficulty is worth the time and effort it will require. So diagnosis is undertaken. It often involves several people, and it always involves the observation of student A as he attempts many reading tasks. The procedure is to try him out extensively on each one of the reading skills that he should have acquired before the present point in time. He undergoes a fairly long test on every reading skill that he should already possess, usually with the teacher or a reading specialist watching him as he does it in order to spot behavioral signs of difficulty. Since he may have several gaps in his learning rather than just one, the testing is continued over all major reading skills. Sometimes the first pass in diagnosis will give no more than a few clues as to the difficulty, indicating points at which more intensive trials are needed.

The conclusions in diagnosis are only tentative because they must be proved. The proving is in the teaching. If the diagnosed difficulties are indeed the gaps in the learning sequence that now handicap the student, the handicap should disappear very rapidly after he learns the missing skills. If it does not disappear, then the diagnosis has been in error or incomplete and there are other gaps not yet discovered—and the process of diagnosis is resumed.

There are good diagnostic tests in reading. This is one school-taught skill that has been intensively studied. More is known about how people learn to read than about any other learning process, and a great deal has been accomplished in discovering the specific steps in the sequence of reading skills. Since it is necessary to know both the skills and the sequence before efforts at diagnosis can be anything but random, the studies of reading have made systematic diagnosis possible in this area to a greater degree than is possible in other fields of learning. Diagnostic tests available in the area of reading, it should be noted, must be used by experienced teachers with special training, and require the expenditure of much time in individual attention to a single child. Even in this most-researched area of learning, there are no short cuts to diagnosis of learning difficulties.

In elementary arithmetic—the learning of the fundamental operations with whole numbers and simple fractions—there is a series of diagnostic tests available. But since the sequence of learning in arithmetic is not so well understood as it is in reading, even this series is more nearly a screening device for preliminary definition of probable difficulties than an instrument for conclusive location of missing skills. Even so, it is very useful in trained hands.

In all other branches of learning except reading and elementary arithmetic, the methods of and instruments for diagnosis of learning difficulties are homemade. As intimated earlier, they consist of trying out the student on all the skills and subskills that are presumed to lead up to the skill he is trying with difficulty to learn now. Any kind of demonstration exercise used in this process is by definition a test— whether it is a standardized test, a teacher-made test, a text, a job devised by the teacher, or an exercise the student himself selects to demonstrate his difficulty. If somewhere in the student's learning background there is something missing, it usually takes many tasks, many tests, to locate the break in learning. And infinite patience.

Testing to Improve Teaching

Accurate judgment of the capacity of students to learn leads to improved teaching, and tests contribute to that judgment. Teaching is improved as it is planned and is aimed toward learnings that students need but do not have—an aiming accomplished in part with tests. Teaching is improved when it is directed and paced to keep step with learning progress, a pacing that is done by testing. And teaching is improved when learning difficulties—gaps in the sequence of learning—are discovered, also a process in which tests are used.

Another important use of tests is in the experimental development of improved teaching techniques. Experimental improvement of teaching has been carried on mostly by teacher-training institutions and by large school systems and has been characterized by patient trial-and-comparison studies, rather than by any large theoretical discoveries or dramatic breakthroughs. Professors and graduate students in education time and again have hypothesized that "students will learn factoring (or vocabulary or grammar or geography facts or whatever) more quickly and permanently if they are taught in this way than if they are taught in the old ways." So they set up a technique for teaching in the new way, persuade some teachers to use the new method for a given period of time, and include similar classes taught in the old ways for the sake of comparison. They test the learners in the experimental classes and in the "control" classes, both before and after the experimental period, to see whether the class taught by the new method did in fact learn significantly more than the classes taught by the old methods. However their experiments turn out, they report their results in the professional journals.

But even when the new method proves to have an advantage nothing short of sensational, as new methods occasionally do, nobody gets very excited about it and nobody promptly throws out the old methods and installs the new. Educators are so conservative in adopting new methods or materials that when a new method of teaching proves to be very promising in an experimental situation, the next likely step is that someone else will repeat the experiment with different students and different teachers in different schools.

After enough experimenters have found the same thing and have reported it in enough journals, the third step is undertaken. The new method is tried in nonexperimental situations by teachers in the "laboratory" schools run by teacher-training institutions for the purpose of demonstrating new techniques and affording supervised practice for teachers in training. One by one, the laboratory schools try out the new method, sometimes improving upon it as they do so; and they report their observations and opinions about it in their journals. When enough experience with the new method shows that it is not only better but completely safe in comparison with older methods, professors begin to teach it and writers to include it in their textbooks in the training of new teachers. And when these teachers, trained at the out-set in the new method, have grown old enough to replace the teachers who once used the older methods—only then is the "new" method used almost universally in schools.

Small wonder that it takes even brilliant improvements forty years to cover the teaching field. And how silly are most of the objections heard when, at the end of this long process, a school describes an important change in method to the PTA. Usually, the parent who complains about "my child being a guinea pig" would find comfort in the fact that the real guinea-pig children who proved out the "new" method when it was still experimental are now fast becoming grand-parents.

Standardized tests may not invariably provide the best criteria for judging the effectiveness of a new teaching technique, but they are nearly always used. They provide evidence of learning wrapped up in a neat package with a number on it; so they have a strong appeal to the researcher whose experiment is both complex and expensive. Obtaining test scores on learners in both control and experimental groups is one of the easiest parts of the whole experiment. Further-more, if the group using the new method learns substantially more or less than the control group and the difference is reflected in aver-age scores on a test that is known, the results seem more credible. "The experimental group using the new method earned a mean score half a grade higher on the *XYZ Achievement Test* than did the con-trol group using traditional methods." This refrain, with variations, is heard constantly in the world of educational research. The dangers that might be inherent in this practice—the chances that a new method might be fobbed off on schools through use of a poor test or the wrong test—are reduced practically to zero because the second and third researchers, the ones who "replicate" the experiment, not only try the method with different teachers and learners but also measure outcomes with different tests.

Testing to Assess Teaching

Administrators, either on their own or at the insistence of parents and school board members, all too often judge the quality of a teacher's instruction by the average of scores earned by that teacher's students on a standardized test. This can be far more dangerous than even the most knowledgeable advocates of educational measurement are likely to know. The danger lies in the fact that it is so easy to accept test results as the only evidence of teaching quality—when, at their best, tests can yield only a small part of the evidence necessary to make a sound judgment. Let us look at some of the things that happen.

A good, carefully built, and widely accepted battery of standardized achievement tests is administered to all eighth-grade students in a city school system near the end of the year. Averages are computed for every class, for every school, and for the system as a whole. If the city-wide averages are mostly higher than the norms developed by the publisher of the tests, a public relations officer may persuade the superintendent to release them to the newspapers with an appropriately modest report. And the temptation may arise to make judgments about the quality of the school system on the basis of the averages alone:

1. We are doing a superior job of teaching reading and the social studies because our average scores are far above the national norm.

2. We are doing a less effective job in arithmetic and science because our averages in these subjects are lower, but we still are not bad because we are above the norms.

3. Any changes we undertake in curriculum or method should be in the areas of arithmetic and science.

4. School A obviously is doing a superb job of teaching reading and English because its averages are a whole year above the high city averages—but what are they doing out at school B, with the same books and teachers' salaries, earning averages below the national norm!

None of the conclusions above is justified on the basis of test scores alone; in fact, these conclusions could be dangerously in error, for the following reasons:

1. In general, children in city school systems do earn higher average scores on achievement tests. Among the reasons is the fact that experienced teachers tend to move into city systems, where salaries are higher. Experienced teachers on the whole are more effective

than inexperienced ones—and the "national norms" with which the city school children are compared include a fairly large proportion of rural and country school children. In other words, one must make sure who is in the comparison group before bragging about being above the norm.

2. Does someone know whether the tests in arithmetic and science fit the system's particular curriculum as well as the tests in reading and social studies? Have the tests been analyzed with this in mind? This school system could be doing a better job in arithmetic and science than in reading, according to its own definition of goals, and still not know it by these results if it has not analyzed the fit of the tests.

3. This much evidence—city averages on one testing—with no supporting evidence or study, is by no means sufficient reason to consider changes in curriculum. Without data to show how much the average youngsters have changed (learned) as a consequence of instruction in each of the measured fields, judging the effectiveness of teaching on the basis of one testing is like judging the winner of a race without knowing whether all runners started at the same place and time.

4. School A and school B cannot be compared in teaching effectiveness until and unless they are first compared in the learning levels at which their students started. If school A's students come from home backgrounds that provide them with rich resources and high motivation in the language arts, for example, the teachers could almost sit back and let nature take its course and the students would still earn a high average on achievement tests in this field. On the other hand, school B might be doing a superb job of teaching, creating impressive changes in students whose home backgrounds are severe handicaps in the language arts.

In some large cities, the population is shifting in character so rapidly that before-and-after studies that cover two or three years are almost totally invalidated by changes in population. During one recent period in Washington, D. C., for example, students from academic and highly motivating home backgrounds were found to be moving at a tremendous rate from the city to the nearby suburbs, being replaced in the schools by children from much less-favored families moving in from rural areas. At the other end of the academic scale, there are some suburban communities—Scarsdale, New York; Oak Park, Illinois; Shaker Heights, Ohio, are examples—where the home backgrounds of "average" children give them such a great advantage academically that their achievement test average scores are too high to be compared with "national norms" at all.

In spite of all their dangers if used unwisely or as single measures, and in the face of the many complications that are a part of a valid evaluation, good standardized tests do contribute a vital part of the information needed to assess the effectiveness of teaching in schools. With proper preparatory work in the schools and the community, with budget and professional help adequate for the job, and with patience and support in the school board, a school system can do a tremendously worthwhile study of its own strengths and weaknesses in the teaching function. Those seriously interested in this evaluative process and wanting to do it well will gain a great deal of insight into the nature of the problem by writing to the Denver Public Schools for the current brochure in the "Denver Looks at Its Schools" series. Denver has a continuing system of self-evaluation in which major parts of the educational job are examined in successive three-year studies; by the time the last study on the schedule is completed, it is time to repeat the first one. Other systems are doing excellent assessment jobs, too; but as a part of its community-information effort, Denver publishes periodic bulletins that are useful to outsiders in understanding the process.

The same considerations as those used with regard to judging the effectiveness of school systems must be made in assessing the individual teacher. Do the tests measure an important part of what the teacher is trying to teach? Does the teacher recognize that they do? Is it known exactly what kinds of pupils the teacher has to teach, his "raw material"? Are there provisions for before-and-after assessment, so that his effectiveness will be judged by the changes he produces? Is the teacher a member of the assessment team, rather than its victim? Unless these critical questions all can be answered clearly in the affirmative, the teacher of bright and academically favored students will look far more effective than the teacher of the less-favored children, whose very real achievements will not be evident.

Use of tests to assess teachers without prior affirmative answers to the above questions almost always produces these specific effects:

1. The good teacher who happens to have students from a less promising academic background is inevitably shown in a bad light. He may be tempted to ask for assignment to a "fast" class which makes a better showing.

2. A good teacher who has had no part in the planning of the assessment, but who discovers that the tests used have different emphases and cover somewhat different topics than are characteristic of his teaching almost invariably drifts into teaching what the test measures—even though his own goals are more appropriate for the students. When this happens, the test is controlling the curriculum in spite of all the courses of study worked out by teachers and supervisors.

3. A good teacher who has imposed upon him an evaluative test that does not well fit what he is trying to teach will, in many subtle and often unconscious ways, enter into a conspiracy with his students to "beat the test." In one way or another, the attitude of the classroom becomes: "If this is what they think is important to test, we'll give it to them, but we'll give it to them by means of quick cramming and intensive before-the-test reviews."

4. A poor teacher in a school where teachers are assessed only by means of an imposed test of the students is protected by the testing. The general coverage and emphasis of many achievement tests are not difficult for a teacher to ascertain, even if the specific questions are closely guarded. The poor teacher can make himself appear a lot better than he would look otherwise by concentrating his teaching just on those things that are likely to turn up in the test, whether they are appropriate for his students or not.

Standardized tests of student achievement are such useful teaching tools that it is often a mistake to try to make them do double duty as measures of the teacher as well. In most schools, it is better not to attempt to have them do double duty, since administrative use of test results to judge teachers usually is less helpful for the students than concentrating on the use of the same tests to aid instruction. But making tests serve both teaching and administrative ends can be accomplished, if:

1. The use of tests as teaching tools is fully accepted by the teachers first, with administrative uses secondary.

2. The teachers are directly and actively involved in planning the teacher-assessment uses of test results.

3. The tests never became clubs over the heads of teachers.

Thus, tests have many uses as tools in teaching. The most important and fruitful uses are those which are concerned with discovering the student's characteristics as a learner, with planning instruction to fit his needs and previous accomplishments, and with keeping close watch on his learning as it progresses so that he will not drop off the track. Secondary uses concern finding the source of trouble when it arises, assisting in research that results in better teaching methods, and in adding somewhat to the assessment of teaching effectiveness. The underlying question in any use of tests is: "How will this use of this test enhance the learning of the students who are my responsibility?" The answers need to be realistic and practical, and they can be.

CHAPTER 7

TESTS IN SELECTION
AND ADMISSION

Since the time of the ancient Egyptians, institutions of higher education have had to exercise some degree of selection among the many who wished to learn. The problem has not lessened over the centuries. Differing attitudes have prevailed toward college admissions in recent years in America, but two general points of view have emerged. These concepts are not opposed—in fact, they often overlap —but most colleges and universities operate according to the philosophy of one or the other. They are:

1. *Selective admission.* The college with a student capacity clearly defined by the limits of budget and plant, but with more applicants than it can accommodate, must somehow select some for admission and turn away the others. The selection should be done in such a way as to assure the best possible education for the greatest possible number of students, meaning that the college should discover those applicants who are best able to profit from the teaching that college has to offer. Such colleges feel strongly that they have not only a right but a responsibility to select students carefully, so that they can utilize their resources of staff and money with the highest rate of return in terms of educational output. The more selective a college is, in general, the fewer students it has who drop out before graduation.

2. *Nonselective admission.* Many state universities and other colleges supported by public funds, by tradition or law, admit nearly all

applicants who have earned a high school diploma within the state. This practice is an expression of the philosophy that every American youngster should "have his chance" at obtaining a college education, regardless of the previous quality of his academic work. This is distinctly an American philosophy, to be contrasted with practices in Europe and elsewhere that begin to close doors to college opportunity for some children at the ages of eleven and twelve. Colleges which admit nearly all who apply quite naturally have high drop-out rates; on the whole, about half of the students who enter nonselective colleges drop out before the end of the sophomore year. It can be said with some truth that in these colleges the selection of students is done after they are admitted. And it can be said with accuracy that almost all nonselective institutions have in the last decade become at least *partially* selective in their admissions procedures—either by making the student near the bottom of his high school class clear special hurdles to get in, or by strongly counseling away from college those whose chances of success appear to be nil.

Arguments grow warm over the relative merits of the selective and nonselective approaches to college admission, but it is likely that both philosophies are appropriate and fruitful. Both philosophies are necessary if this nation is to have at one time collegiate institutions which devote their total energy to the intellectual development of the gifted few and institutions which offer opportunity for college education to every young citizen without regard to his earlier decisions or circumstances.

The background of interactions that accounts for the phenomenon of increasing selectivity is complex and really cannot be described in generalizations, but the symptoms of the trend are simple and easy to see:

1. Many colleges that twenty years ago had to recruit actively to fill their freshman classes now are setting up fairly rigorous admission requirements and using tests in the selection of students from among applicants, who outnumber the available places.

2. Many colleges that for years had been completely nonselective in admissions for philosophical or legal reasons—mostly colleges and universities supported out of public funds—now are employing selec-

tive procedures that more or less prevent students at the bottom of the ladder in academic ability from using up college space and facilities in an obviously hopeless try at higher education.

3. Some colleges that do not need to be very selective in admission, because their candidate group barely outnumbers the class they can accommodate, are applying noticeably more rigorous admissions standards anyway—gambling on the probability that higher admissions requirements will in time attract applicants who are more talented academically.

4. All of these colleges in transition from low or no selectivity to a higher level of selectivity in admissions are using tests for tactical as well as educational purposes, that is, as part of a planned movement to improve the position of the institution in its effort better to educate young people.

But why must we give tests for admission to college in our time? Having taught and counseled and tested the student for three or four years, why cannot the high school submit enough evidence to support the admissions decision—without having the colleges insist on tests of their own before a candidate is admitted or rejected? Do the colleges not trust the high schools? Do they not believe what the high school transcript says about a student? The answer to these questions lies not in any shortcoming of the schools, nor in any lack of faith on the part of the colleges, but in a problem of communication that cannot be avoided in the American system of education.

There are more than twenty thousand high schools in the country and, because by tradition public education is controlled and molded by citizens in local groups, no two of those high schools are identical. The tradition of local control of education means that each high school attempts to respond to the wants and needs of its own community, selects its own teachers, sets its own values in the assignment of marks, often tailors its curriculum to its own students and their environment. To students who move and have to change high schools, the differences between schools are dramatic.

Yet, to the college admissions officer, the transcript of grades from one high school looks very much like the transcript from any other. An A average earned in a highly academic high school where most graduates go on to college may mean something quite different from an A average earned in a high school where academic learning is secondary to vocational training. With candidates' transcripts coming from as many as a thousand different high schools each year, however, the college admissions officer has no infallible way of knowing what the reported grades mean. Lacking a method for interpreting the information sent to him about the candidates for admission, he needs some means for deciding which are the ones most likely to succeed in the studies offered by his college.

Admissions tests can be used to help the college interpret the information it receives from high schools about students applying for admission. The performance of an applicant on a test given to all applicants has some meaning that is not contained in any of the other records about him. His test score is the one piece of evidence about him that is most nearly comparable with similar evidence about all the other candidates. The test is a common denominator that permits the college to make allowances for differences among schools and communities. Each youngster taking the test has a chance to "show his stuff" in direct competition with all other applicants, in a way that disregards how well he gets along with teachers, what kinds of marks he has earned, and what kind of school he comes from.

When the admissions officer has before him the transcript and recommendation of an applicant and the record of his independent performance on a standard learning job (the test score), he can obtain real meaning from the transcript even if it comes from an unknown high school. He may reflect, for example: "This youngster ranked in the middle of his large graduating class but did better than 95 per cent of other applicants on the admissions test; so he's more competent academically than his record indicates. Either that is a 'tough' high school in terms of competition for marks or this applicant wasn't working up to his capacity." Or: "This applicant is valedictorian in a small rural school but scores quite low on the admissions test; either his test performance was untypical for some reason or his grades have been earned in an 'easier league.' "

In either case, the addition of test information has given the admissions officer a different source of insight into the learning characteristics of the applicant, insight which he could not have applied to the admissions decision on the basis of the transcript alone. And the admissions officer uses the test performance information with the high school record—not instead of it—in reaching his decision about each applicant.

Every year more than a million young people graduate from twenty-odd thousand high schools and enroll in more than two thousand colleges. Since every one of these students is an individual and different from all other students, since every high school is different from all other high schools, and since every college is different from all other colleges, the process of getting the right student to the right college most of the time is complicated. Parents fidget as Junior approaches the college-choosing age. High school principals turn gray prematurely. All because college admissions tests are given.

Admissions Tests Used by Highly Selective Colleges

The term "highly selective" applied to a college does not mean necessarily that it selects better students than other colleges, but that it has more applicants to choose from, in proportion to the number of places available, than most other colleges. It means that for every student who can be admitted there are at least three or four—sometimes as many as twenty—who apply for admission. And most of the applicants are good students. Some educators describe these institutions as having *competitive* admissions procedures. There are about fifty colleges like this, such as Harvard College, California Institute of Technology, Stanford, and Massachusetts Institute of Technology. They are, for the most part, "prestige" colleges with wide reputations and a drawing power that reaches all over the world. These colleges are virtually all members of the College Entrance Examination Board and require applicants to take at least one of the Board tests as part of the admissions process. The procedure goes something like this:

The student who is interested in going to one of the highly selective colleges, together with his parents and the high school counselor, ideally should begin to consider college possibilities during the student's sophomore year. If his grades are good and his school test record indicates that he handles the tools of academic learning well, the counselor may suggest that together they gather as much information as they can about whatever particular college the student has in mind and also look into other "possibilities." The counselor has some well-known references to start with: the *College Blue Book* and the College Board's own *College Handbook,* in which each of the several hundred member colleges has written a description of its student body, curriculum, and campus life. He also recommends that the student should plan to take the College Board's *Preliminary Scholastic Aptitude Test* during the fall of his junior year, to get an idea as early as possible whether his expectations for going to a highly selective college are realistic. The student and his parents now have a lot of reading and thinking and talking to do. They may not have realized that there are so many good colleges, nor that there is such a wealth of information about them in print.

The student, whom we shall name Fred for convenience, takes the *Preliminary Scholastic Aptitude Test* (PSAT) one morning in October of his junior year. The test takes two hours and covers two major kinds of academic skill by verbal material and mathematical questions. Although the questions themselves are completely different from one test to the next, the following sections quoted from the 1963 *PSAT Bulletin for Students* indicate what the test is like.

The sample questions that follow illustrate the kinds of questions that you will find in the PSAT. The questions in the verbal section test your ability to understand word relationships and to comprehend what you read. Those in the mathematical section test your ability to understand and solve problems. The explanations following the questions are intended to indicate to you the proper way to approach and solve the questions.

Verbal section

The verbal section of the PSAT has four kinds of questions: antonyms, sentence completions, analogies, and reading comprehension. Each type is described and illustrated in the following sections.

Antonyms (opposites). These questions are designed to test the extent and quality of your vocabulary. In each question a word is given, and you are asked to select from the five choices that follow it the one most nearly opposite in meaning. The vocabulary used in this section includes words most high school students should have met in their general reading, although some of the words may not be ones you use in your everyday speech.

The test directions for this kind of question are as follows:

Each question below consists of a word printed in capital letters, followed by five words or phrases lettered A through E. Choose the lettered word or phrase which is most nearly *opposite* in meaning to the word in capital letters.

Since some of the questions require you to distinguish fine shades of meaning, be sure to consider all the choices before deciding which one is best.

1. AGILE:
   (A) humble   (B) clumsy   (C) useless   (D) timid   (E) ugly

Since "agile" means quick, dexterous, and easy in movement, the best answer is "clumsy" (B), which means slow, awkward, and ungainly in movement. If you know the meaning of this word, answers (A), (C), (D), and (E) are obviously incorrect. This is a relatively easy question.

2. ALLEVIATE:
   (A) lower   (B) aggravate   (C) finish   (D) control   (E) amuse

This is a relatively difficult question. "Alleviate" means to lighten or lessen (usually physical or mental troubles). The meaning most nearly opposite is "aggravate" (B). To one who understands the meaning of "alleviate," (C) and (E) are obviously incorrect. "Control" (D) can be thought of in relation to physical or mental troubles, but the act of controlling would not provide the opposite of "lightening or lessening"; the correct answer must imply increasing or magnifying. "Lower" (A) in a sense carries the same meaning as "alleviate" but is much more general and is certainly not the *opposite* of that word.

Sentence completions. Sentence completion questions require you to complete a sentence from which one or two words have been removed. They provide a measure of one aspect of reading comprehension: your ability to select a word or phrase that is consistent in logic and style with other elements in the sentence. If you understand the implications of the sentence, you will be able to select the one answer that best fulfills its meaning.

The sentences cover a wide variety of topics of the sort you are likely to have encountered in your general reading. Your understanding of the sentences will not depend on specialized knowledge in science, literature, music, philosophy, the social sciences, or other such fields. Still, a broad general knowledge of a wide range of topics should be helpful.

The directions given for sentence completion questions are as follows:

Each of the sentences below has one or more blank spaces, each blank indicating that a word has been omitted. Beneath the sentence are five lettered words or sets of words. You are to choose the one word or set of words which, when inserted in the sentence, *best* fits in with the meaning of the sentence as a whole.

3. Where the world is going is of no particular concern to him; that it.................... is sufficient.
   (A) flourishes (B) acts (C) moves (D) grows (E) triumphs

The problem here is to select the word which most clearly conveys a lack of concern about "where the world is going." "Moves" (C) is the best choice, for it does not imply direction. Each of the other terms, by suggesting an interest in more than mere movement, indicates more concern than (C) does.

4. .... makes it possible for us to profit by the experience of past generations as if this experience were our own.
   (A) Language (B) Democracy (C) Progress (D) Truth
   (E) Economy

This relatively difficult sentence completion requires some understanding of one important function of language, namely, that it enables us to profit by the experience of past generations. Notice that if (B), (C), (D), or (E) were to be fitted into the blank space, they would fit no better than their opposites. That is, we can profit from the experience of past dictatorships as well as from past democracies. Falsehood has its lessons as well as Truth. Thus there is nothing particularly *fitting* about any of the choices except "Language" (A). Lacking a language, it would be almost impossible for one generation to communicate with another. Given a language, the experiences of Democracy, Progress, Truth, or Economy—or their opposites—of one generation can be used by a succeeding one.

Analogies. Analogy questions test your understanding of relationships among words and ideas. They ask you to analyze such relationships and to recognize those that are similar or parallel in nature. Some of the questions will involve cause and effect relationships; in others you will be asked to carry an analogy from a concrete, tangible relationship to an abstract, less tangible one. You should consider each relationship critically and then select as your answer the choice that comes closest to satisfying all of the demands.

The directions given for analogy questions are as follows:

In each of the following questions, a related pair of words or phrases is followed by five lettered pairs of words or phrases. Select the lettered pair which best expresses a relationship similar to that expressed in the original pair.

   5.   FOOTBALL : SPORT ::
      (A) frame : picture   (B) clock : time   (C) gourmet : food
      (D) cherry : fruit   (E) intelligence : personality

This is a relatively easy analogy. Since football is one of a number of sports, the correct answer must involve some object that is included in a larger category described by the second part of the answer. The choice that best fits this description is (D), "cherry : fruit."

   6.   ILLEGIBLE : WRITING ::
      (A) obnoxious : odor   (B) iridescent : glass   (C) soundproof : wall
      (D) illusory : sight   (E) garbled : speech

This is an analogy of medium difficulty. Since writing that is illegible cannot be read, the correct answer must involve terms that result in an inability to comprehend something. Choice (E) is the only one that expresses a similar relationship: garbled speech cannot be understood.

Reading comprehension. Because of the importance that colleges place on their students' ability to read with understanding, insight, and discrimination, approximately half the time on the verbal section of the PSAT is devoted to measures of reading comprehension. The prose excerpts used in the test come from a variety of fields, such as history, the social sciences, physical science, biological science, music, art, literature, and philosophy.

You will be tested in reading comprehension at several levels. Some of the questions will test your understanding of the plain sense of what has been directly stated. To answer other questions, you must be able to interpret and analyze what you have read. Still other questions are designed to test your ability to recognize reasonable applications of the principles or opinions expressed by the author. And some of the questions require you to judge what you have read—to observe good and bad points in the presentation, to recognize how far the author has supported his statements by evidence, and to recognize and evaluate the means used by the author to get his points across.

The directions for reading comprehension questions are as follows:

Each passage in this group is followed by questions based on its content. After reading a passage, choose the best answer to each question. Answer all questions following a passage on the basis of what is *stated* or *implied* in that passage.

(The passages for this test have been adapted from published material to provide the student with significant problems for analysis and evaluation. The ideas contained in the passages are those of the original author and do not necessarily represent the opinions of the College Entrance Examination Board or Educational Testing Service.)

Here is a sample passage.

Talking with a young man about success and a career, Doctor Samuel Johnson advised the youth "to know something about everything and everything about something." The advice was good—in Doctor Johnson's day, when London was like an isolated village and it took a week to get the news from Paris, Rome, or Berlin. Today, if a man were to take all knowledge for his province and try to know something about everything, the allotment of time would give one minute to each subject, and soon the youth would flit from topic to topic as a butterfly from flower to flower; life would be as evanescent as the butterfly that lives for the present honey and moment. Today commercial, literary, or inventive success means concentration.

7. The author implies that a modern scientist
   (A) makes discoveries by accident
   (B) must bend his mind in a specific direction
   (C) is able to contribute only if he has a background of general knowledge
   (D) must be well versed in the arts
   (E) must be successful, whatever the cost

This is a "plain-sense" question. The author gives Dr. Johnson's view, which he says was good in Dr. Johnson's day, and then gives his own view of what is true today. He says that success in a particular field—science, as well as any other—today demands concentration within that field. The answer, then, is (B). Some students answer (C); but (C) is true of Dr. Johnson's view and is directly contrary to the author's.

Question 8 is harder, but still requires only an understanding of the plain sense of the selection.

8. According to the passage, if we tried now to follow Doctor Johnson's advice, we would
   (A) lead a more worthwhile life
   (B) have a slower-paced, more peaceful, and more productive life

    (C) fail in our attempts
    (D) hasten the progress of civilization
    (E) perceive a deeper reality

The author has tried to show that it is impossible today to follow Dr. Johnson's advice; in one minute per topic, no one could learn much of anything. So the answer to question 8 is (C). Some students answer (B) and some answer (D); however, the author nowhere implies that we could or should turn the clock back. These may be the students' own views, but the question is not asking for them.

  9. Which of the following sayings best reflects Doctor Johnson's advice?
    (A) "Be a Jack-of-all-trades and master of none."
    (B) "Make education a career."
    (C) "Know what you know well."
    (D) "Be a Jack-of-all-trades and master of one."
    (E) "The race is to the swift."

Doctor Johnson advised the youth "to know something about everything"; that is, he should try to know a little bit in every field of knowledge. Of the choices, only (A) and (D) suggest this idea by advising one to be a "Jack-of-all-trades." But Doctor Johnson also urged the youth to know everything about something; that is, he should try to master some one subject. This counsel is expressed only in (D) in the phrase, "master of one." Therefore, (D) is the correct answer.

Mathematical section

Some questions in the mathematical section require you to apply graphical, spatial, numerical, symbolical, and logical techniques to situations already familiar to you; these may be similar to exercises in your textbooks. In other- questions you are presented with novel situations and are called upon to do original thinking and problem-solving. You will not be expected to use mathematical knowledge beyond elementary algebra or the geometry implied by the formulas printed for your reference at the beginning of each mathematical section of the test. Although no specific knowledge of subject matter beyond that just described is required, well-taught courses in mathematics preceding and following the ninth grade will probably improve your performance on the PSAT and will provide a stronger foundation for your college-level work.

    Following are the test directions and reference formulas that appear in the mathematical section of the PSAT.

In this section, solve each problem, using any available space on the page for scratchwork. Then select the *one* correct answer.

The following information is for your reference in solving some of the problems:

Circle:

  area $= \pi r^2$
  circumference $= 2\pi r$
  degrees of arc in a circle $= 360°$

Straight angle measures $180°$

Triangle:

  sum of the measures of the angles of a triangle $= 180°$. If CD is perpendicular to AB, then

  (1) area of $\triangle ABC = \dfrac{\overline{AB} \times \overline{CD}}{2}$

  (2) $\overline{AC}^2 = \overline{AD}^2 + \overline{DC}^2$

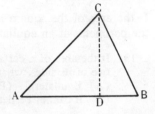

Definitions of symbols:

  $<$ means "is less than"; $>$ means "is greater than";
  $\leqq$ means "is less than or equal to"; $\geqq$ means "is greater than or equal to";
  $\perp$ means "is perpendicular to"; $\parallel$ means "is parallel to."

Note: Figures accompanying problems are not necessarily drawn to scale and are assumed to lie in the plane unless otherwise stated.

The sample questions provided below illustrate the types of problems and the range of difficulty that may be expected in the PSAT.

10. If there are P girls and R boys in a class, what is the ratio of the number of girls to the total number of boys and girls in the class?

  (A) $\dfrac{P - R}{P + R}$ (B) $\dfrac{P}{P + R}$ (C) $\dfrac{P}{R}$ (D) $\dfrac{R}{P}$ (E) $\dfrac{P + R}{P}$

This question requires the construction of a ratio. One might first think of the answer in this form: $\dfrac{\text{girls}}{\text{class}}$ and then in this form: $\dfrac{\text{girls}}{\text{girls} + \text{boys}}$. Direct letter substitution gives us: $\dfrac{P}{P + R}$

11. City R is 200 miles directly east of city T, and city H is 150 miles directly north of T. Assuming the cities lie in a plane, what is the shortest distance in miles between H and R?

  (A) $50\sqrt{7}$ (B) 175   (C) 250   (D) 300   (E) 350

This question involves the Pythagorean Theorem and the recognition of a right triangle. It is easiest if one sees that the ratio $\frac{150}{200}$ is the same as $\frac{3}{4}$, thus making this a 3–4–5 type of right triangle. This immediately gives one a 150–200–250 right triangle.

12. A square and an equilateral triangle have equal perimeters. What is the length of a side of the triangle if the area of the square is 9?
    (A) 3 (B) 4 (C) 6 (D) 9 (E) 12

If the area of the square is 9, its side is 3 and its perimeter is 12. If the perimeter of an equilateral triangle is also 12, its side is 4.

13. If the area of a certain triangle is equal to one-half the product of two of its sides, what kind of triangle is it?
    (A) Equilateral (B) Acute (C) Right (D) Obtuse
    (E) It cannot be determined from the information given.

The answer is (C). If the area of a triangle is one-half the product of two sides, one side must serve as the base and the other side as the altitude. This occurs only in the case of the two legs of a right triangle.

14. If an arrow ($\rightarrow$) between two expressions indicates that the expression on the right exceeds the expression on the left by 1, then which of the following is (are) true?
    I. $x^2 \rightarrow (x+1)^2$

    II. $\dfrac{x}{y} \rightarrow \dfrac{x+1}{y+1}$

    III. $x(x+2) \rightarrow (x+1)^2$

    (A) None (B) I only (C) II only (D) III only (E) I and II

In this question, you must work with a new symbol that has been defined. In cases I and III the right expressions must be expanded before comparison. In I, the right member exceeds the left by $2x + 1$. In II, the right member exceeds the left by $\dfrac{y-x}{y(y+1)}$. In III, the right member exceeds the left by 1, making (D) the correct answer.

15. If rain is falling at the rate of 2 inches per hour, how many inches of rain will fall in x *minutes*?
    (A) $\dfrac{1}{30x}$ (B) $\dfrac{x}{30}$ (C) $\dfrac{30}{x}$ (D) $\dfrac{60}{x}$ (E) $30x$

In this question, it is essential to realize that either the rate must be changed to inches per minute or the time to hours. Thus, rate in inches per minute $\left(\dfrac{2}{60}\right)$ times x, the time in minutes, or rate in inches per hour (2) times $\dfrac{x}{60}$, the time in hours, yield the same result of $\dfrac{2x}{60} = \dfrac{x}{30}$ inches of rain.

16. If the radius of circle X is 40% of the radius of circle Y, the area of circle X is what per cent of the area of circle Y?
(A) 16   (B) 20   (C) 40   (D) 80   (E) 160

If the radius of circle Y is R, that of circle X is .4R. Therefore, the area of circle Y is πR^2 and of circle X is $.16\pi R^2$. The per cent is $\dfrac{.16\pi R^2}{\pi R^2} \times 100 = 16$.

Directions: Each of the questions below is followed by two statements, labeled (1) and (2), in which certain data are given. In these questions you do not actually have to compute an answer, but rather you have to decide whether the data given in the statements are *sufficient* for answering the question. Using the data given in the statements *plus* your knowledge of mathematics and everyday facts (such as the number of days in July), you are to blacken the space on the answer sheet under

(A) if statement (1) ALONE is sufficient but statement (2) alone is not sufficient to answer the question asked,

(B) if statement (2) ALONE is sufficient but statement (1) alone is not sufficient to answer the question asked,

(C) if BOTH statements (1) and (2) TOGETHER are sufficient to answer the question asked, but NEITHER statement ALONE is sufficient,

(D) if EACH statement is sufficient by itself to answer the question asked,

(E) if statement (1) and (2) TOGETHER are NOT sufficient to answer the question asked and additional data specific to the problem are needed.

17. Which side of △RST is the longest?
(1) ∠S measures 52°, ∠T measures 38°
(2) ∠R is a right angle.

By using statement (1), it may be inferred that ∠R measures 180° — 52° — 38° or 90°. Therefore side ST is the longest because it is the hypotenuse. By using statement (2), it may be inferred immediately that side ST is the hypotenuse and therefore the longest. Since each statement is sufficient by itself to answer the question, the correct answer is (D).

18. If x and y are positive integers, is x + y odd?
   (1) xy = 12
   (2) x — y is odd.

By using statement (1), it may be inferred that x and y must be factors of 12. Therefore, x and y could be 12 and 1, 3 and 4, or 6 and 2. In the first two cases, one of them is even and the other odd, and x + y is odd; in the third case, both are even and x + y is even. Thus statement (1) alone is not sufficient to answer the question asked. By using statement (2), it may be inferred that x and y cannot both be even or both odd since then x — y would be even. Since x — y is odd, one of them must be even and the other one odd and the question can be answered "yes." Since statement (2) alone is sufficient but statement (1) alone is not sufficient to answer the question asked, the correct answer is (B).*

Fred's PSAT answer sheet is returned for scoring to Educational Testing Service, which develops and administers the PSAT for the College Board. In December, Fred's scores are returned to the school. To give them meaning, they are reported on a score scale extending from 20 to 80—essentially the same as the score scale for the *Scholastic Aptitude Test,* but without the last digit. Along with the scores, for Fred and for the school, come bulletins that will help him and the counselor to use the scores in deciding about college.

Another useful source of information is the *Manual of Freshman Class Profiles,* which contains statistical descriptions of the freshman classes at more than two hundred Board member colleges. Comparing Fred's PSAT scores (verbal and mathematical) with scores on similar tests earned by students in the freshman classes of these listed colleges, the high school counselor gives Fred and his parents an idea of the academic competition he could expect to face in each of the colleges he has in mind.

They find, for example, that in the college which is Fred's particular favorite, his test scores match those of students who are now in approximately the middle of the freshman class. He becomes at-

* *Bulletin for Students, 1963 Preliminary Scholastic Aptitude Test,* College Entrance Examination Board, pp. 7–17.

tracted to two other possibilities through discussions with the counselor and by poring over their catalogues, and finds that his scores are a little better than the average of the freshman class in both cases. At his father's Alma Mater, however, which his father is promoting heavily at home, Fred's scores rank in the lower third of scores earned by entering freshmen, which might indicate that Fred would find himself under heavy academic pressure in the attempt to keep pace with his classmates.

All in all, Fred and his parents have received some useful and revealing information to consider in the process of making final choices. By autumn Fred has decided that he definitely does want to apply to the college he originally favored (college *A*), but one of the colleges he has learned about from the counselor and his own investigations sounds almost equally promising (college *B*), and he intends at least to make a good stab at getting into his father's college (college *C*). He sends for applications from each of the colleges and receives a number of instructions.

College *A* (the leading choice) tells him to return his application form as soon as possible, asking his principal to attach a transcript of course grades and a confidential recommendation, and also to take the College Board *Scholastic Aptitude Test* in the December administration. College *B* (the "dark horse") suggests that he take the SAT in December or January, plus the *Writing Sample* and his own choice of the College Board's mathematics tests, intermediate or advanced. College *C* (his father's Alma Mater) requires four College Board tests—the SAT, the *English Composition Test,* one of the mathematics achievement tests, and either the *Writing Sample* or another achievement test—at any or several of the Board's testing dates in December, January, or March.

The best way to fill the requirements of all three colleges seems to be to:

1. Take the Board tests at their December administration, since this testing date is required by college *A* and permitted by both of the others.

2. Take the tests at the Board testing center nearest his home, in the high school of the next town, eight miles away.

3. Take the following Board tests:

a. The *Scholastic Aptitude Test* (SAT), required by all three colleges
b. The *Writing Sample,* required by college *B*
c. The *English Composition Test,* required by college *C*
d. The *Intermediate Mathematics Test,* required by college *B*

The *Writing Sample* and the *Intermediate Mathematics Test* would satisfy the requirement of college *C* that he take it or a second achievement test in addition to the *English Composition Test*—it said so in the college catalogue. Thus in one day, and at one place, near his home, Fred will be able to take the entrance examinations for three different widely separated colleges. He mails off his test application and his father's check to cover the examination fees.

Having completed his registration for the College Board tests he needs to take, Fred turns his attention, when he can, to getting ready for them. He has received a free copy of *A Description of the College Board Scholastic Aptitude Test* from his school counselor. In it, he is happy to note that the questions and problems in the *Scholastic Aptitude Test* are very much like the questions and problems in the PSAT, which he took eight months ago. No problem of understanding what the SAT is all about.

From his counselor, Fred obtains a copy of *A Description of the College Board Achievement Tests.* In it, he finds certain paragraphs to have particular interest:

Most of the Achievement Tests measure your command of factual information: in languages, knowledge of vocabulary and syntax; in the sciences, familiarity with scientific terms, processes, and concepts; in mathematics, mastery of a large body of basic material and operations; in history and the social sciences, a knowledge of United States and European history and of certain important historical, political, and economic concepts.

Each College Board Achievement Test measures not only your knowledge of the facts about a particular subject but your ability to reason with these facts in order to solve problems appropriate to the subject. Because courses vary widely from school to school, the questions selected for any test necessarily must be suitable for students attending a wide variety of schools. . . .

Facts are the basic materials with which you must work in any subject-matter area. But simply "cramming in the facts" is not likely to result in your getting a good score on a test. To do well, you must have learned how to think with the facts you know. This kind of ability does not come overnight. It comes from patient, conscientious effort throughout the school year in the classroom, in library and laboratory, and at home. In each subject, the goal of your effort should be an increased familiarity with all sorts of problems and an increased ability to deal with them thoughtfully and accurately.

Where no specific facts are called for, as in the English Composition Test, practice in the kinds of skills the tests require is vital. Though you do not, for example, need to know the terminology of grammar to do well on this test, you will profit from a wide background of reading and extensive practice in writing. . . .

Since both your knowledge and your ability to use this knowledge are tested, it would be a mistake for you to assume that mere practice with objective types of questions will result in high scores. Practice with objective tests is helpful to the degree that it acquaints you with the kinds of questions used and with the process of taking multiple-choice tests. Familiarity with the method of testing, however, is not a substitute for familiarity with the subject tested.

In short, the knowledge you have accumulated in the classroom and elsewhere is basic to good test performance. The best possible preparation for the tests is your regular schedule of study, reading, writing, classroom discussion, and classroom examinations.*

For practice, Fred works through the sample exercises from the *English Composition Test* and decides that he will ask his English teacher to explain some of them to him—they look tough. He works through the sample problems in mathematics and confirms his earlier decision to take the intermediate mathematics test rather than the advanced one. Then he goes back to read again certain paragraphs from the description of the *Writing Sample:*

The Writing Sample, as its name suggests, is an essay-writing exercise which provides colleges with direct evidence of your competence in written expression. You are given one hour to write an essay on a single assigned topic, and copies of your essay, exactly as written, are sent to your school and to the colleges you specify at the time you write the essay.

The essay will not be graded by the College Board. It will be used by the college to supplement the information provided by your school grades in English, your score on the English Composition Test (if you are asked to take it), and any other evidence that may be submitted relating to your writing ability (such as teachers' recommendations or ratings).

* *A Description of the College Board Achievement Tests,* 1963 Edition, College Entrance Examination Board.

Here is an example of the kind of topic you will be asked to write on if you are requested by a college to take the Writing Sample:

Loyalty is a quality which, in the abstract, we delight to honor. In practice, however, it is something that may vary with circumstances and conditions. There is "loyalty among thieves," "loyalty to self-interest," "loyalty to a pal at the expense of truth," as well as "loyalty to an ideal, to country, or to cause."

Define your concept of loyalty and arrive at a principle regarding its use or abuse.

Directions: Express your ideas in a well-planned essay of 300 to 500 words, using several paragraphs to organize your discussion. Your point of view should be supported by and illustrated from your own experience, or by appropriate references to your reading, study, or observation. Be specific. You are expected to express your best thought in your best natural manner. After you have written your essay, *underline the sentence* which you think comes closest to *summarizing your central idea.*

On the sheet containing the topic and directions you will have space to do "scratch work," but you are cautioned against attempting to write a draft of your essay on this sheet because you will not have time to copy such a draft on the paper provided for your essay.

In writing your essay on the special paper provided, you will automatically produce four carbon copies in addition to the original copy. (To make certain that all the copies are legible, you should maintain a firm pressure on your pen while writing your essay.) The original copy of the essay will be sent to your school, as will any carbon copies on which you have not printed the name and address of a college. Each of the other copies will be sent to the college that you specify on it. It is to your interest to specify the names and addresses of these colleges at the time you write the essay.*

About a month before his testing date, Fred receives from the College Board his tickets of admission to the testing center for December. They contain his name, the place where he is to take the tests, the times of the morning and afternoon sessions, the names of the tests he is to take, and his registration number.

After the great day has come and gone, answer sheets are sent off the same day, via air mail, to Educational Testing Service in Princeton, New Jersey, where, along with the test papers of nearly half a million other candidates, they will be scored and reported.

Fred's answer sheets are scanned and scored with the use of high-speed electronic equipment, and quality control checks are made to

* *Ibid.,* pp. 12-13.

insure that there is no error in scoring. The scores are fed into a computer, which adds them to the information supplied on his test registration card and at the same time "searches" for scores he may have earned on earlier College Board tests in earlier administrations. The scores are reported on a three-digit scale that runs from 200 to 800 and that has remained quite constant in meaning since 1942. This is the "College Board Scale." On this scale, Fred has earned scores of 520 on the SAT Verbal, 584 on the SAT Mathematical, 495 on the *English Composition Test,* and 588 on the *Intermediate Mathematics Test.* A report card, bearing Fred's name, the code number of his high school, his examination number, the date of his examination, and all of his test scores, is sent to colleges *A, B,* and *C* according to the instructions Fred noted on his test registration form. Shortly after scores have been reported to the colleges, they are also reported back to the high school, so that the school may know how well Fred has done and inform him. All this takes five to six weeks from the day of his testing.

Fred's essay, written at the request of college *B* and called the *Writing Sample,* has four carbon copies under the original; one carbon is sent to college *B,* one to college *C,* and the original and remaining carbon copies are sent to Fred's high school. Students who take College Board tests other than the *Writing Sample* may at any time later—sometimes many years later—pay a look-up fee and request to have their scores reported to any institution of higher learning.

What is done with Fred's scores when they reach the colleges he has designated?

At college *A,* Fred's application form, the transcript of his high school record, and the handwritten recommendation of his principal have been in a file folder bearing his name for several months, waiting for his SAT scores to arrive. When the SAT scores for candidates tested in December arrive, Fred's among them, the admissions officer immediately does a preliminary tabulation of the verbal and quantitative scores of all the candidates of this year for college *A* and makes a graph that looks like the one in Figure 8. Then he calls together the official college admissions committee, which in a college of this kind may be composed of several interested and experienced professors, the registrar, and himself as chairman. He reports that while the college will continue to admit 200 new freshmen per year, there are already 410 candidates for admission who have completed the application forms and have reported test scores. He shows them the graph and notes that the distributions of scores are very similar in average and in spread to distributions for applicant groups in each of several previous years. With this general picture of the candidate group as a whole, the committee settles down to the long, hard job of considering in depth the individual characteristics of every student for whom they have a folder. Meeting at least two hours every day, it

FIGURE 8

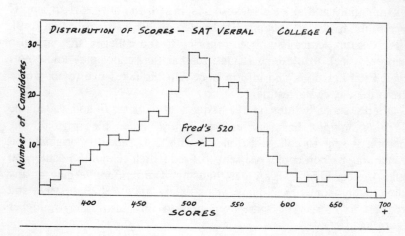

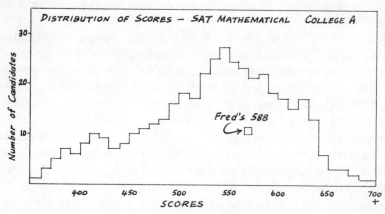

takes them more than a week to sort the candidates into three categories: admit, not admit, and borderline.

Applicants in the "admit" category for college *A* are those whose high school grades have been good to excellent, whose test performance on the SAT has earned one score above 500 and the other no less than 400 (this is a private and very flexible criterion), and whose principal's recommendation indicates worthy character. Applicants in the "not admit" group are those whose total records indicate clearly that they are likely to be unsuccessful and unhappy at college *A*. This leaves a fairly large number of applicants in an "undetermined" category—candidates whose high school records are notably less impressive than their test scores (possibly a symptom of lack of effort) and whose principals' comments also indicate ability without much drive, candidates with borderline records both in school and on the test, and candidates with high school grades but very low test scores, and candidates with records containing some other information that raises doubts in the minds of the committee member as to the suitability of the college for the student.

At this point, the work of the admissions committee comes into closer focus. They have no way of knowing how many of the candidates in their "admit" category have college *A* in mind as their first choice and actually will turn up in the fall—or how many of them have applied to college *A* as "insurance" and would actually enroll in some other college if admitted. So, using their experience as a guide, they decide to send letters of "provisional admission" to about 280 candidates and "waiting list" letters to 60 others, expecting that out of those admitted they will obtain close to 200 freshmen for the places they have. The balance will be admitted from the waiting list. There is always something of a gamble; they could come out a few short or, worse yet, a few over their capacity. But things generally adjust themselves; so they take the chance.

There are 205 candidate folders in the admit pile (Fred's among them), consisting of the records of students whose high school records and test scores clearly indicate that they have good chances of succeeding in college *A*. Since 205 admissions are not enough to fill the freshman class, however, the committee must select 75 more from its pile of 131 folders in the borderline category. Again they review every case in the group, arguing, compromising, deciding. The committee member whose vote put a student in the borderline group in the first place may be called upon to defend his position. In the end they agree, more or less, on the 75 borderline candidates to be added to the admit category.

The admissions officer then writes a warm letter to Fred and 279 other high school seniors, saying that if he keeps up his grades until the end of the year, and still merits the recommendation of his principal, college *A* will be happy indeed to welcome him as a new student next fall. When the letter arrives, Fred and his parents are so pleased that they go out for dinner to celebrate.

College *B,* which Fred chose after reading about it and talking with the counselor, is the farthest from home, but it is a good small liberal arts college with a considerable number of its graduates in mathematics and humanities going on into advanced work. Fred's *Writing Sample* arrives at the college at about the same time as his College Board test scores. The chairman of the English department receives it and gives it to a member of his faculty. Each *Writing Sample* is read by at least two professors.

The dean of students has already studied the applicants' high school records and recommendations and made notes on them. When the test scores arrive, the mathematics department looks over the mathematics scores, while the admissions officer familiarizes himself with the SAT scores. By the time the admissions committee (which typically may include the heads of all departments, the dean of students, and the admissions officer who doubles as registrar) meets, each member is briefed on some aspect of the candidate's record.

College *B* can admit 160 freshmen next fall, and it has the formal applications of 425 students who seek admission. Experience indicates that about 240 candidates should be "accepted" to assure a class of 160. The job of the committee is to choose those 240 out of 425 who are most likely to gain the greatest good from four years of study at college *B.* They have a method, slow but effective, for doing this.

The admissions officer opens the discussion of each candidate. He considers the grade average information in the high school record and the two SAT scores. On the basis of long experience he estimates that Fred would have a slightly better than 50–50 chance of earning a B average in the nonmathematical courses and about 80 chances out of 100 of making at least a C average. In mathematics courses he is not likely to do quite so well because of the high standards of mathematics in college *B*. In this college, then, Fred is obviously not expected to turn in a brilliant performance, but a respectable one.

Then it is the turn of the dean of students. He has studied Fred's high school record with care. He reports that while Fred's total high school grade average for three years is merely good, his grades earned in the junior year are substantially higher than the earlier ones —indicating perhaps an awakening of interest in academic learning or some increase in effort. He quotes the principal's recommendation in that part which mentions that as a junior Fred has apparently "buckled down" to school work with some signs of zest.

The head of the mathematics department confirms that Fred looks as if he would be acceptable so long as he did not hope to excel as a mathematics major. Even though Fred's score on the College Board *Intermediate Mathematics Test* was 588, or better than about 80 per cent of the select group of students who took the test, the mathematics department at college *B* attracts so many able students with four years of rigorous high school mathematics that the merely good student is not likely to be able to compete in a major program in this subject.

Then the head of the English department speaks up. "This boy looks pretty 'average' for college *B* on all counts so far, but I would like to enter a special word in his favor. His essay, read by two others in my department as well as by me, contains some interesting ideas very well expressed. The sheer mechanics of language were not outstanding, but there are several passages in his six paragraphs that indicate a real skill in expression—a skill I'd like to see developed. If no one else objects, I will vote for putting him in the 'accept' category."

So Fred receives another letter of provisional acceptance from college *B,* stating the same conditions about senior year grades as the letter from college *A,* but adding the notation that the Department of English found special merit in his essay. Fred begins to feel like a sought-after college man, and shows it a little.

College *C* is the Alma Mater of Fred's father. It is a well-known prestige college, but it does not much resemble the college from which he graduated twenty-four years ago. In his day, it was in large part a "family college," admitting a high proportion of sons and grandsons of alumni, accepting the "gentleman's C" as routine, and encouraging social life and intercollegiate athletics. At that time, almost every applicant who appeared to fit the familiar pattern and could afford the tuition and living costs was admitted.

But time, the war, and a president with high aspirations for the college began to change all that shortly after Fred's father graduated. By now, nearly a third of the students at college C are supported at least in part by academic scholarships, the faculty is composed of scholars eminent in their fields, a "gentleman's C" automatically evokes a pointed invitation to talk with the dean, and members of the football team must maintain high academic averages. There are, each year, nearly five thousand applicants for admission to a fresh-man class that can accommodate no more than one thousand students.

The admissions office combines Fred's two SAT scores with his high school grades in a formula that gives about equal weight to grades and test scores, then computes a predictive index for Fred, based on the academic success of previous students who have had high school records and test scores similar to Fred's. This double-barreled index is an estimate of the odds favoring his successful work in mathematics-science courses and in English and social studies courses. A card reporting this information is added to Fred's folder.

The admissions committee at college C is proud of its tradition of providing a full and personal reading of the papers of every candidate, no matter how great the numbers may be. No candidate is ever turned away "automatically" or screened out by a procedure in which his record is not read carefully by a responsible member of the faculty. With five thousand applications, however, the committee must divide up its work and assign first readings of a certain number of applications to individual members. Fred's folder is read by a professor of political science who has been reading records like Fred's at college C for eleven years.

The professor of political science reads the high school transcript first, recalling that one of the best students he ever had came from this high school seven years or so before. Then he reads the principal's hand-written comments; Fred obviously is a nice lad and a fairly good student. There is a note in the folder from Fred's father in which he owns to his special interest in having Fred attend college C and delicately mentions his fund-raising activities in the local chapter of the alumni association. There is also a note from Fred's pastor, attesting to his character, and another short letter from his high school basketball coach, describing his sportsmanship and devotion to practice. Finally, he looks at the predictive indexes computed from grades and tests by the admissions office—like most of his colleagues on the committee, he leaves this bit of information until last in his study of each applicant to avoid any possibility that it might prejudice his own personal assessment of the raw information. The cold facts of the matter are that two thousand of this year's candidates, half the applicant group, have earned substantially higher grade averages than Fred. Twenty-five hundred of them have earned higher test scores. This college is in the academic major league and must say to many youngsters like Fred: "Your record shows that you are a fine young person and a good student, but among the thousands applying for admission here there are more than we can take of fine young people who are even better students. You are likely to be more successful and a lot happier at some other good college." Phrased as tactfully as highly tactful educators can say it, this is the message that goes back to Fred from college C.

There is no celebration when this letter arrives. Fred has shooting pains in his ego for about eight hours, and his father glumly wonders if his work in the alumni association has been worthwhile after all, but in a day or two the message that college C wants to convey is both understood and accepted. On the whole, to earn admission to selective colleges, young people these days have to be better students than their parents were and must have achieved better records in high school.

The case of Fred illustrates in a general way the methods used by three different selective colleges in applying knowledge gained through testing to the process of admitting students. No two colleges use exactly the same methods. Nor do any number of colleges depend upon test scores to precisely the same degree. In the most sophisticated admissions procedures, test scores are used almost wholly to interpret the other kinds of information obtained about each candidate. In almost all colleges, test information is, in one way or another, combined with the high school records of the student in reaching a decision about his admission. Extremely few of the selective colleges use test scores alone, even for preliminary screening. This is as it should be, for test scores provide only one indication of what a student is like and what he can do.

The tests developed by the College Board are designed for college applicants in a "fast league," but some six hundred colleges now require all candidates for admission to take one or more of the Board's tests. This number includes virtually all of the highly selective institutions, except a tiny handful that continue to use their own testing procedures. The American College Testing Program was recently established to meet the placement, guidance, and admissions-testing needs of those state colleges and universities which in the past have not been selective. The ACT procedure is set up to provide a standard service quickly and with a minimum of expense, while the Board's program is set up to provide a varied and flexible testing service under the most "secure" conditions.

Admissions Tests Used by Nonselective Colleges

All accredited colleges are selective in certain important ways. Some of the publicly supported institutions which admit all graduates of accredited high schools within their own state borders apply extremely selective standards in admitting students from out of state. Others apply admissions criteria that vary from year to year according to the budget and the capacity of the college in relation to the applicant group. Still others, notably the universities of Michigan and Minnesota, have developed cooperative arrangements with the state's high schools that accomplish the effect of highly selective admission through practical guidance of students while they are still in high school. Tests of various kinds are used at some point in virtually all methods of selection.

Almost all the colleges in Minnesota, of which there are more than thirty, including public and private, subscribe to and support the Minnesota State-wide High School Testing Program. This is a cooperative venture with a successful history of more than thirty years in which one program of testing, paid for by the colleges, provides both the test information the colleges need for admissions and the test information the high schools need for academic guidance of students. The University of Minnesota is the operating agent for the program, but its policies are determined by a permanent committee composed of representatives of all the colleges and of the high schools. The system is voluntary as far as the high schools are concerned, but school participation runs close to 100 per cent because the advantages for the schools are obvious.

The Minnesota steering committee lays out its testing schedule and content several years in advance, so that everyone knows exactly what is coming. Each year, there is a basic group of tests which the committee hopes all schools will administer to all their juniors—usually tests of general academic ability, achievement in English, and achievement in mathematics or science. In addition, each year there are provided other and more specialized tests, such as subject matter achievement measures, personal inventories, and interest batteries, which the school is encouraged to use at little or no cost. These tests are shipped to the schools, administered there by the students' own teachers and counselors, and returned to the university center for scoring and reporting. Students' scores are reported back to the high schools for guidance use, with carbon copies of the scores on the basic program tests sent to all Minnesota colleges participating in the system. Each test score thus reported shows how the individual student compares with all other students of his grade in the state. It is a percentile rank score that describes the student's comparative location among a representative hundred of other students who took the same test.

The Minnesota testing program has several benefits that are of particular interest to educators in other states. Most of the graduates of Minnesota high schools who go on to college attend colleges within the state; the testing for admission to any of them is done at one time, as a regular part of the high school schedule, in a way that is known to and convenient for nearly everyone concerned. This testing is at least as useful to the students and the high schools as it is to the colleges. Since the schools administer the tests and the university serves as a central agency for supplying materials and scoring services, the program costs the colleges only a modest amount and costs the student nothing. As important as anything is the fact that every year Minnesota samples its entire population of high school juniors with measures of academic skill and accomplishment, sharing results with all the educators in the state who have an interest in the further schooling of young people. By the end of his junior year, every Minnesota high school student who shows academic promise, whether he has plans to go to college or not, has heard from at least one college that he does have skills he should continue to develop—an encouragement toward higher education which often is more impressive, and effective, than encouragements given by the student's own teachers and counselors.

Of course, since the Minnesota program alerts all colleges to the fact that certain named students are unusually competent a year and a half before they are of college age, it sharpens somewhat the competition among the colleges for the better students. Colleges write to the high schools and ask for the transcripts of students the colleges had never heard of until the roster of test scores arrived. In this respect, the Minnesota testing program gives the colleges somewhat the same kind of "scouting" ability to locate and encourage good students as many colleges have had for years to locate and encourage good halfbacks.

No two Minnesota colleges use the test scores in the same way. Some of them have established "cutting scores." Some set general criteria for admission, such as "top half of the graduating class in grade average and top third in test scores"—and require an applicant who cannot meet these criteria to present a special case for himself. Others combine test scores with high school grades in formulas that experience has shown to be most predictive of success in their own institutions.

The university, which is in some respects a kind of mother institution for all other colleges in the state, has large counseling resources that are available to all Minnesota youth. The student who applies for admission to the university with a high grade average and high test scores has little trouble getting in. The student who applies with a low grade average or low test scores, or both, is invited to see a university counselor as soon as he can; he is given names of counselors and counseling hours and telephone numbers, so that he can find his way to counsel if he is unused to large institutions. After the appointment is made, the counselor obtains from all their various sources all the kinds of information about the student that exist—grades, extracurricular interests, school counselor's folder of notes, test scores, everything—and studies all of them. He is likely to chat by telephone with the student's high school counselor or principal. His job is not to tell the student what to do—and this surprises many students and parents whose expectations are that they will be told what to do— but rather to bring together a great deal of information about the student and a great deal of information about the colleges in the state, and to help the student make his own decisions on the basis of full information.

During the interview, the student reviews his high school and test record with the counselor. Then they turn to information about colleges. They match what they know about the student with what they know about each college and establish for the student a sort of table of odds: "With my high school record and my test scores [the student can say to himself] the odds are 60 out of 100 that I'll make a passing grade at college X, 70 out of 100 that I'll survive at college Y, and 80 out of 100 that I'll be able to stay in college Z—unless I change my habits radically and suddenly become a wholly different kind of a student than I've been for the last four years." The good counselor neither encourages nor discourages the unrealistically ambitious student; he just equips him with the facts and reminds him of the importance of making a sound decision. This is true whether the counseling is done by the counselor in the student's own high school or by a university counselor.

In some ways, this system of admission by guidance thrusts the student into the making of a tremendously important adult decision about himself at a much earlier age than the system in which an admissions committee decides for the applicant whether he should be allowed to undertake study at a particular institution. It becomes the student's own decision to enter a particular kind of intellectual competition, and his job is to survive the selection that takes place after the freshman class is enrolled. There is much to be said in favor of both systems.

The tests used in the admission process by nonselective colleges are distinguished by their variety. The instruments used in the Minnesota testing program mentioned earlier in this chapter are a combination of standardized tests available commercially and tests devised by the university especially for this program. With a highly organized and successful program that covers the whole state every year, the committee operating the Minnesota program take advantage of their excellent opportunity to build and validate new instruments of their own as they go along.

Almost every commercially available test of academic ability and subject matter achievement is used somewhere, by some college, as a means of obtaining information to be used in the admissions decision. For twenty years, the single test used by more colleges than all others was the *American Council on Education Psychological Examination,* which is not psychological at all, but a measure of academic skills of verbal and mathematical kinds. The *Ohio State Psychological Examination,* also widely used in admissions during the same period, is also a test of academic skill, stressing almost wholly the verbal kinds of learning. Both of these tests, though now superseded by more recent and more sophisticated instruments, continue to serve many colleges well in admissions work.

There is almost certain to be no one "best" test for all colleges. This situation is chiefly a reflection of the almost infinite variety among colleges as well as among students. Surely, the admissions testing of all colleges could be accomplished with far fewer kinds of tests than are now used—our free enterprise society encourages competition among test-makers as well as among automobile-makers— but it is likely that a number of different tests and testing programs will be used to meet the needs of all colleges and all applicants.

The testing techniques of the nonselective colleges vary even more than the tests they use. Minnesota, with its one master testing program serving all colleges in the state, is almost unique. By far the greatest number of nonselective colleges use test scores obtained not in any coordinated program at all, but received directly from the high schools. Many of them will ask the high school of an applicant simply to "include with the transcript of grades a record of the test scores earned by this student, making sure that the names of the tests are clearly indicated"—and then use as best they can the assorted test scores thus accumulated. There are even some colleges that will mail an objective test directly to the applicant whose record is innocent of test scores and request that he set up his own honor-bound testing period and return the completed test to the college as soon as possible. Again, the variety of methods is almost infinite, but in every case the object of the test for admission is to give the applicant a chance to perform on a standard set of problems that the college knows and can interpret.

Tests Used in the Award of Scholarships

All of the tests previously mentioned as instruments used in the process of admitting students to college are used also in the process of selecting the students to whom scholarship aid is to be given. While it is true that some scholarship funds have been established for the educational aid of students deemed to be "deserving"—or of students who are the children of employees of a particular company, or of students who have demonstrated a special interest in a certain field of study—and use tests not at all in the selection of recipients, an overwhelming majority of scholarship grants require candidates for scholarship money to demonstrate their capacity for college education by taking a test. In other words, the student who seeks the aid of scholarship funds in furthering his education must indicate that he is "deserving" and that he has ability to benefit by the education the scholarship money will pay for.

Since there are two quite distinct practices that bear the name "college scholarship program" in many places, it will be wise here to define and describe them separately. The first is the traditional practice of many colleges to arrange some kind of financial assistance for students who have already been admitted and are pursuing their studies successfully, but who encounter financial difficulties that might force them to drop out of college if aid could not be obtained. Financial assistance of this nature, for students already enrolled, is variously called a "grant in aid," "student loan," or "scholarship."

The second practice bearing the same name has to do with discovery and encouragement of, and offers of needed financial assistance from sources outside the college to, especially promising students before they are admitted to any college. Technically, the first named practices are called "college scholarships" and the second kind are called "sponsored scholarships." This chapter is concerned primarily with sponsored scholarships.

Fortunately for students, the tests used most often for the purpose of sponsored scholarship awards are the same tests used for college admissions—so the scores a student earned in taking the test for college admission can often be used in consideration of his application for scholarship aid and he does not then have to take a second test for scholarship purposes. This two-way stretch of several widely used admissions tests saves time, effort, and countless dollars. One test frequently used as partial evidence in awards of scholarships is the *Scholastic Aptitude Test* of the College Board. The test is sufficiently difficult to discriminate among the most able students, its security against leaks, frauds, and cheating resembles that of the vault at Fort Knox, its scores have meaning in colleges all over the country, and— best of all—over a million college-bound youngsters take it every year, anyway, for regular college admission purposes. Many donors of large and small scholarships simply ask that candidates for awards submit SAT scores, earned in the senior year of high school, along with transcripts and other evidence of academic promise. Although there are increasing numbers of scholarships awarded by independent agencies, such as foundations, industrial companies, labor unions, and churches, the large majority of scholarships are awarded by the colleges themselves; and they, of course, use the same test scores that they use for admissions.

Tests other than the SAT are of course widely used in the selection of scholarship winners. Notable among them is the *National Merit Scholarship Qualification Test,* much mentioned in the press each year at the time it is given and at the time scholarships are awarded. The NMSQT is the examination administered by a corporate body organized for the purpose of locating the most promising students to be beneficiaries of scholarships awarded by a large group of industrial and philanthropic donors. The NMSQT is used principally as an instrument for locating scholarship winners; so it is taken in addition to any other tests the student may take for purposes of college admission. The NMSQT is a vast screening device, identifying large numbers of academically able students who are then called "semi-finalists" and are asked to take the College Board's SAT to "confirm" their NMSQT scores.

With scholarships, as in other forms of selection, it must be kept in mind that very seldom do test scores decide the winners. The student's score on a test may qualify him for consideration, or help him to certify that he is a good investment risk as a college student, or attest that he belongs in the big league where scholarships are given out—but almost never will he, rather than another student, be awarded a scholarship just because his test score is a few points higher. After the candidates' ability to justify scholarship aid by good work in college has been predicted on the basis of high school records and performances on tests, these kinds of evidence usually are set aside; and the awards are made on the basis of additional important characteristics: initiative, independence, creativity, leadership, character, and so on. It is a revelation to see the scholarship committee, often composed of the top officers of a giant corporation, study the large amount of information necessary in order to make good judgments regarding these qualities.

One important characteristic of modern scholarship selection is only remotely related to testing. This is the "award commensurate with need" principle, in which funds for scholarship aid are made available to a larger number of students by being tailored to their needs rather than by being awarded in stated amounts regardless of need. It works this way: When a student applies for scholarship aid, his parents are asked to turn in a statement of financial status much like an income tax return, which is coded and treated with the utmost confidence. If the student's high school record, recommendations, and test performance earn him a scholarship award, the decision to make the award is made first, followed by the decision as to the amount of the award. Although the conditions relating to scholarship awards differ, the size of the stipend generally is adjusted to the capacity of the family to pay for the student's college education. If the scholarship-winning student is a member of a family which is easily capable of paying his way, the student receives the honor and the certificate of the award, notices in the newspapers, and the other social recognitions of his accomplishment, but his financial return is a token amount of perhaps $100. The student winner whose family resources just cannot support college costs at all receives recognition and maximum financial support as defined by the donor. In this way, the able youngster who qualifies for scholarship aid receives recognition regardless of his family's financial resources, but the principal part of the scholarship money is used to aid able students who need it most. Not all scholarship funds are administered in this way, by any means, but an increasing proportion of the total scholarship sources in the country is applied on the principle of need.

Several agencies collect and interpret information for use in determining the amount of money needed, but the pioneering group in this field has been the College Scholarship Service of the College Entrance Examination Board.

Tests Used in the Placement of College Students

Speaking generally, "placement" involves the selection or assignment of particular courses and curriculums, taking into account the student's previous achievement, his weaknesses, and his aspirations. It is wasteful of time, and often destructive of interest, to assign a student to courses that are simply "repeats" of courses he has already passed with success in high school. On the other hand, it is almost always academically fatal to assign a student to a course that is far beyond his level of present achievement, assuming him to have learnings that he does not possess.

Proper placement of entering students is increasing in importance because of the increasing diversity in the previous educational experience of students—a diversity which cannot be untangled by study of the high school transcript. For example, a high school transcript entry—"Biology, 1 year, average grade B"—could mean a good introductory course in botany, zoology, personal hygiene, health; a mediocre course in any one of these areas; or a very high-level course, such as one of those taught in the Biological Sciences Curriculum Study design. There is reason to believe that all of the experimental developments in the secondary school curriculum—in biology, in mathematics, in physics, in chemistry—as well as the courses developed under the Advanced Placement Program, have the effect of increasing the diversity of precollege training and presenting colleges with a much more difficult placement problem.

Colleges have found the placement problem most pressing (or at least the most widespread) in the fields of learning where the student's period of study has been long and fairly continuous—English, mathematics, foreign languages. Some students arrive with a complete command of the mechanics of the language and are ready for advanced courses in English; others need the usual freshman English course, while still others lack basic skills and should take remedial work. They certainly do not all belong in the same course. Neither do they all belong in the same mathematics course, or at the same level of foreign language instruction, for they differ a great deal in both experience and skill. This is where tests, on-the-job demonstrations, help in the sorting of students into courses.

If the tests administered to applicants for admission have included tests in subject matter mastery, the college has placement information about the admitted student before he arrives on campus. In the case of Fred, for example, college *B* required him to take the College Board's *Writing Sample* and a mathematics test in addition to the SAT. College *B* also has his score on the *English Composition Test* and the *Intermediate Mathematics Test,* which he took for admission to other colleges. All of the test scores and the *Writing Sample* will be used for placement—in fact, his interesting *Writing Sample* helped make his admission certain—but his placement in English will be based also on his score on the *English Composition Test* and the verbal section of the *Scholastic Aptitude Test.* Together they indicate that he has both the ability and the background in English to proceed with the regular freshman English course and need not spend time on mechanics and grammar. His ability and attainment in mathematics indicate that he should begin at an intermediate level, since he does not need a refresher course in high school mathematics but is not ready for a calculus course. All this can be done realistically and fairly accurately by using the knowledge the college has of him before he actually arrives.

In many colleges, testing for student placement is done after the freshman arrives on campus. Often there is a special period of several days before the upperclassmen arrive—sometimes called "Freshman Week"—in which new students are introduced to campus life and sit through sessions of placement testing. The common pattern of this period calls for the testing to be done on the first or second day, followed by a day or two of familiarization with the campus and special social activities, and a culmination in which each student sits down with a faculty adviser to consider his plans and make out his course program. On the basis of his test performance in competition with all the other freshmen, he is assigned to one of the English courses: English I (mostly grammar), English II (half grammar and half composition), English III (half composition and half survey of literature), or English IV (all literature). In some cases, if his performance has shown real strength, he may be allowed the choice of omitting all of the freshman courses in English and starting off with the sophomore course in composition or speech. The same general pattern of deciding and locating takes place with respect to the foreign language courses, the mathematics sequence, and, in many fewer cases, other freshman subjects.

The tests used in the on-campus administrations for placement purposes usually are of several kinds: Commercially available standardized tests are used when their content and emphasis clearly parallel the course offerings of the college; departmental tests—made by the faculty to cover their course content—often are used to supplement the standardized instruments; College Board Placement Tests are used where they fit the curriculum; and almost always an essay examination is given to permit the English department to sample the student's skill in organizing and expressing his ideas.

The "reference group" with which a new student's score on a placement test is compared always is composed of students who have taken the courses in question *in that college*. The principle involved is simple and straightforward: If an entering student can earn as good a score on a valid achievement test for College Algebra 101 as most students who have taken the course, there is no real need to have him take College Algebra 101. His education will be better advanced by having him start his college mathematics course sequence at a higher level. There are many differences from college to college in the use of placement tests, but this principle remains basic. The tests are used to help the student demonstrate the levels of learning he has already achieved—in comparison with earlier students in that same college—and thus to help him avoid repeating work he has already mastered. Of course, placement test scores work in the other direction, too. By comparison of the new student's test performance with the performances of other students who have taken particular courses, it is possible to help the new student to avoid taking a course that is too advanced for him.

A notable development of recent years in the whole area of college placement is the Advanced Placement Program, a project of the College Entrance Examination Board. This is a cooperative program in which certain high schools have set up some courses at the college level for their most able students, and those students at the end of such instruction have taken special examinations to earn college credits at certain colleges. In this way, outstanding students from high schools able to offer college-level instruction can enter college at the normal age with advanced standing in terms of college credits already earned. More than one-fourth of all the colleges in the country use the Advanced Placement Program in some way to place and give credit to able young men and women who have undertaken studies of college caliber before entering college. The examinations are prepared by committees of college professors and secondary school teachers and cover the subject matter of typical college freshman courses. The typical *Advanced Placement Examination* includes about two hours of essay questions, requiring the student to formulate his own solutions to the problems presented, and about one hour of objective questions. As one example of the impact, in the fall of 1960, approximately one hundred new students entered Harvard as sophomores, directly out of high school. The impact of the idea involved in advanced placement in college, its effect in freeing able students from what has been termed the academic lock step, is likely to be enormous and is only beginning. Its success will depend about equally upon school-college cooperation and upon skill in making tests that measure college learning.

Tests Used for Admission to Advanced Studies and Professional Fields

All of this chapter thus far has been concerned with testing for admission to, and placement in, college. In terms of the numbers of students affected, this proportionately large emphasis on college-admission testing probably is appropriate. But there are equally important points of admission both above and below the college freshman level, although smaller numbers are involved. For example, there is a Secondary School Admission Testing Program, operated by and for a group of highly selective preparatory schools, which looks very much like a "little College Board" and offers an annual program of tests at centers all over the country—for youngsters in the sixth to eleventh grades whose parents hope to enter them in the independent secondary schools. And, for another example, there are the U.S. Department of State *Foreign Service Examinations,* for assistance in the selection of foreign service officers for the Department of State.

There is too little space in the chapter even to list the programs for selection and admission in which formal testing plays an important part. Some of the tests for selection, evaluation, or even accreditation, include:

1. *Graduate Record Examinations*—to assist admissions officers in appraising the academic fitness and preparation of applicants for graduate study in arts and sciences

2. *Law School Admission Test*—to provide information about the mental abilities and educational attainments of candidates for the study of law

3. *Admission Test for Graduate Study in Business*—to measure mental abilities related to success in the study of business at the graduate level

4. *Chartered Life Underwriter Examinations*—to assist in the certification of chartered life underwriters

5. *American Board of Surgery Test*—to assist the American Board of Surgery in evaluating the qualifications of surgeons who desire certification by it

6. *National Teacher Examinations*—to aid school boards and administrators in selective recruitment of teachers for employment

Conclusion

This chapter has dealt with problems of admissions at considerable length because the social pressures of our time involve so many American families in emotional experiences of no little moment as college-going time approaches for their children. The whole topic of college choice and the competition for admission has received such extensive treatment in the press, sometimes accurate and sometimes not, that a kind of misinformed folklore has grown up around the testing aspect of the process. Some of those who have spoken most often in public print have succeeded only in creating a false aura of witchcraft about the whole business. It is hard to conceive an idea more distantly removed from the supernatural, however, than testing for admission to institutions of higher learning. It is concerned rather with the realistic attempt to match individuals with the colleges and programs where they will be most effective and which will contribute most to the further development of their abilities.

CHAPTER 8

TESTS
IN GUIDANCE

Older people have been giving advice and guidance to the young for many centuries, but the field of guidance in education is still only about one generation old. Its definitions as well as its practices are still in the process of initial development. The role of the guidance counselor—and the role of the classroom teacher in guidance functions—in the school are not yet clearly seen by many educators. The training required for certification of counselors has not yet been decided in many states. Specialists in guidance themselves are still hard at work on the kinds of study and discussion that lead toward the "professionalization" of the specialty. With all its newness and its lack of final definition, however, school guidance has proved its worth where it has been properly established and certainly will enlarge its effect on the education of young people.

The counseling of students on personal and social matters, an important part of every guidance person's work, is the subject of a substantial body of professional literature. Since this aspect of guidance is seldom related to the tests schools give, however, it is not covered in these pages.

The process of education in the United States is unlike that in most European countries in several important respects, one of which involves the choices open to students as they mature. In our system, the student is offered a number of choices about himself and his career as he progresses through school, choices which he is encouraged and, it is hoped, equipped to make himself. In fact, from the junior high school up through the graduate school (a span of about twelve years), our system provides an almost continuous reminder of and preparation for the making of personal choices by the student —choices of next things to learn, of vocations to consider, of curriculums to follow, of colleges or training schools to attend, of professions to enter. The system also provides enough flexibility to permit changes of direction when students discover that they have made mistaken choices or come upon additional information that makes modification of earlier choices desirable. The variety and number of choices open to the student are distinctively characteristics of American education, as is the freedom of the student to make the choices himself. Almost without exception, the educational systems of other nations in the Western culture have only one or two choice points in the career of the student, and almost always the choices are made for him by someone else.

There are certain points on the educational ladder where choices are especially numerous and particularly important:

1. *The junior high school period* (grades 6–9). At this level of schooling, the student is completing learning of fundamental academic skills and is getting ready for the departmentalized and subject-concentrated studies of the high school. During this period, he and his parents need to reach at least tentative conclusions about what his high school education will be like. Will it be wholly academic, aimed at preparation for college? Will it be mostly vocational, aimed at preparation for a job right after graduation from high school? Will it be a combination of vocational and academic studies, aimed at keeping choices open for later decision?

2. *The senior high school period* (grades 10–12). At this level of schooling, the student is faced with the final decision about continuing his formal education after high school or going to work, if he has postponed this decision. If he has already made the decision to continue schooling, he should decide by the end of his twelfth year (preferably by the end of the eleventh) which college or institute he intends to go to, and for what purpose. If he has decided to go to work after high school, he should decide what kind of work he prefers and where to look for it.

3. *The junior college period* (freshman and sophomore years). During the first two years at the college level, whether the institution is a two-year junior college, a private four-year liberal arts college, or a large state university, the student still has many choices open to him. Should he terminate his formal education after two years of college? Should he begin a specialization in the junior year? If so, which one and where? Should he press on for four years of liberal education? If so, what should be his major concentration in the last two years? What vocational or professional goals beckon now?

There are other points in education around which student choices cluster—vocational choices in the junior college or decisions on graduate training, for example—but the three listed above affect more people than the others and will serve adequately to illustrate the role played by tests in making choices.

Testing in Guidance at the Junior High School Level

Most children entering the sixth and seventh grades are unaware that they are approaching choice points. A part of the guidance program in all good junior high schools, whether that program is carried on by classroom teachers or by guidance specialists, is devoted to informing youngsters about the kinds of decisions that are creeping up on them and to preparing them to make informed judgments. Toward these ends, most junior high school students are helped to make three kinds of preliminary explorations:

1. What am I like? What are my interests, both in school and out of school? What kinds of hopes and aspirations do I have for myself, in the work I want eventually to do, and in the way I want to live? Am I consciously working toward these things I want, or am I waiting for them to happen? What are my strengths and weaknesses in school work? What kinds of things am I especially good at? What kinds of adults do I admire and imitate? Do I want to change the kind of person I am? If so, how?

2. What is high school like? How is it different from elementary school and junior high school? Will I find it easy or hard? What different kinds of courses are offered in the high school I will go to? Which of these courses should I take? Why?

3. What is working for a living like? What kinds of jobs are there for people like me? How well will I like working in them? How well will I succeed in them? Do I need to make decisions now for any of them? What is the training like for jobs that interest me? Are there some jobs that I should cross off my list of possibilities? Are there some that definitely should be near the top of my list?

In the exploration of "What am I like?" the student is introduced to his school record, the history of his victories and defeats in the school job. Here is objective evidence about "What have I been like?" which, presented in the right way, helps most students to begin building an understanding of themselves. Children in their early teens usually appear to be able to see meanings in their records and to generalize from those meanings. Presented with neither praise nor censure, the student's own record has for him a relatively objective interest that resembles his interest in snapshots of himself at earlier ages. Here is how he has looked to eyes other than his own. Here is a mirror he has not used before.

An especially interesting part of the student's school record is the notation of his test scores—if they are represented in a way he can interpret. Aptitude and achievement test scores are of special interest to him because they portray an assessment of his skills and his accomplishments that is not contaminated by what the teachers think of him —an angle particularly important to boys. Students are quick to note and comment on achievement test scores in the record that are at variance with teachers' grades in the same subject, especially if the test scores are higher than the grades, and the fact that the variance exists tells them something. When scores on tests of learning ability and achievement are consistently higher than teachers' grades, the youngster almost invariably volunteers: "I sure could work a lot harder than I do on my school work." Or: "I don't gain much when I give the teacher a bad time." And almost always the record of test scores confirms the things the student has suspected about himself in the way of school learning—"I'm better in math than I am in social studies"—building in him some confidence that the school is not only interested in him but also is not altogether blind in its assessment of him.

Then there are tests given especially at this period to give him a current assessment of his school learnings. These tests give the student the chance to improve his assessment of what he is like now by comparing his test score profile with the profiles of what he has been like before. The consistency of this record, the presence or absence of dramatic changes from year to year, often brings the student closer to realization that the skills he is learning in school are best acquired by steady effort and attention rather than by sporadic bursts of steam or frequent turnings over of new leaves.

A sample of the kinds of things a student sees in his test record as an eighth-grader may be observed in Figure 9. In this school, percentile ranks in the publisher's norming group are recorded as numbers, and then the individual's percentile rank is graphed in the quarter in which it falls in comparison with the publisher's grade group (Publishers' Norms). George probably looks first at the highs and the lows. What are they? His general learning ability scores in comparison with those of the children in the publisher's group are high (top quarter) in the primary grades, then level off at a lower level, although they are still a little above average. Ability scores on the quantitative side moved into the top quarter and stayed there; achievement scores in arithmetic have been in the top quarter all along. Reading skills started high but dropped to about average. Writing and listening scores started above average but have gone down with the years. Science has stayed a little above average and social studies a little below. Comparing his scores with others earned in his own school (School Grade Norms), George notes that he is below his grade average in reading, writing, listening, science, and social studies.

With some help from the counselor, George sees the pattern and meaning in these things. He started out in school with learning skills better developed than a majority of other youngsters, and he has forged right ahead in his arithmetic learnings, maintaining his lead over the average students and even increasing it some—but look at what has happened to his language skills. He has lost ground. He never did like English very well, and he did just enough of the grammar work to get by with the teachers. He likes science and has always worked quite hard in science classes, but look where his science achievement tests scores are! Do you suppose that his lag in reading and writing skills is preventing him from getting the most out of science and is keeping his science scores down?

FIGURE 9

BENJAMIN FRANKLIN SCHOOL

Test Record of: *George A. Smith*

SCHOOL GRADE NORMS (25% / 50% / 75%)	PUBLISHERS' NORMS (25% / 50% / 75%)	Category	Subtest	GRADE	TEST	Publishers' Norm value
		LEARNING ABILITY TESTS	General	1	K-A Form A	65
				2	K-A Form B	80
				4	SCAT – 4A	70
				6	SCAT – 4B	66
				8	SCAT – 3A	74
			Verbal	4	SCAT – 4A	55
				6	SCAT – 4B	45
				8	SCAT – 3A	44
			Quantitative	4	SCAT – 4A	75
				6	SCAT – 4B	82
				8	SCAT – 3A	86
		READING SKILL		2	Metropoliton-Prim.1	80
				3	Stanford-Elem.K	78
				4	Stanford-Elem.L	65
				6	Stanford-Int.K	45
				8	STEP – 3A	55
		ARITHMETIC SKILL		4	Stanford-Elem.L	78
				6	Stanford-Int.K	90
				8	STEP – 3A	95
		LANGUAGE ARTS	Writing	4	Stanford-Elem.L	55
				6	STEP – 4A	40
				8	STEP – 3A	21
			Listening	6	STEP – 4A	55
				8	STEP – 3A	45
		SCIENCE		6	STEP – 4A	70
				8	STEP – 3A	60
		SOCIAL STUDIES		6	STEP – 4A	45
				8	STEP – 3A	35

George comes back later for another look at his records of tests and grades, finally asking if he can make a copy of the test record to take home. What has George thinking, and slightly worried, is that for years he has thought he wanted to be some kind of scientist when he grows up—he likes math and science, doesn't he?—but now he realizes that he may have a shortcoming that could stand in the way of being a scientist: reading and writing. Of course, George and his parents have been told this very thing since he was in the fourth grade, but now George begins to see it himself, and suddenly it has both meaning and importance. He not only makes out his ninth-grade study program with a resolve to bear down in English, but also asks his parents to find out about possibilities for some tutoring in English during the summer. This is a new George, a maturing one, a George with new insights stimulated by the evidence provided by tests.

Not all teen-agers see these things in the record themselves, of course. For those who do not or cannot, the counselor points out the implications of performance in the past for performance in the future. The girl who has constantly done poorly in English is advised to consider whether she would get much out of Latin in the ninth grade. The boy with grease under his fingernails and a top test performance year after year in arithmetic achievement (though with a spotty record of teachers' marks in arithmetic) is urged to take the "tough" sequence in academic mathematics rather than the general mathematics course that terminates in tenth grade.

Along with study of their test and class records, students in eighth and ninth grades often explore and discuss and reflect on their interests. What kinds of things interest me most in school? What kinds of things out of school? Have my out-of-school interests any relationship to my in-school interests? Do my interests have any bearing on the courses I should take in high school? On my choice of a career?

Some children at this age are quite able to analyze their interests and to generalize about them. "I get along pretty well in all school work, but the things that really get me interested and working hard all are related to knowing people—history, and biographies, and English literature and things like that." Or: "I like reading and especially writing and have saved all the poems I have ever written." Or: "School work is all right, but what I think about whenever I can—and read about it, too—is mechanics and customizing cars and making hot rods." Or: "Animals are what I like best, especially wild animals, so I read about them a lot and go out into the woods whenever I can."

Other children have not thought about their interests and cannot generalize about them. If other youngsters of their circle begin to generalize about their interests, some of the slower-starters will, too; but not all of them.

Interest Inventories as Counseling Aids in Junior High Schools

For those whose recognition of their own interests is well defined, as well as for those who have never thought about them, the use of some formal inventory of interests is helpful. There are several available to the school. In some of them the questions are quite direct: "Do you like (dislike, don't care) to take a broken lock apart to see what is wrong with it?" In others, the questions may be more indirect: "With which one of the following groups of people would you like most to spend an afternoon?" In these inventories, there are no "right" or "wrong" answers; the scores represent summations of interests in various kinds of activities and vocations, but they have no connotations of good or bad. So must students work through the interest inventories feeling no pressure at all.

At this junior high school level, student interests are studied and discussed not to define or measure or evaluate or categorize them in any specific way, but to make sure that each student is aware of his interests, can think about them in a fairly objective way, and can start to see the relationships that will always exist between his interests, abilities, and schooling, and his eventual choice of life work. This is a part of knowing one's self that is taught to most youngsters in the junior high school, and the interest inventories are useful instruments in the teaching. Children are much better able to answer the question "What am I like?" at the end of the junior high school period not only because they are more mature, but because the school has gone to considerable effort to help them find out.

As a student approaches high school, it is important for him to have at least given thought to his own interests. Does he have any? Do they match his abilities? Do they have a pattern or are they scattered and unrelated? Do they suggest areas of study heretofore not thought of? Are they interests that correspond to adult vocations or are they all avocational? Are any of them likely to lead to a more concentrated interest in the next few years? Do they betray the fact that a person's interest most often is greatest in the things he knows best?

The most widely used inventories of interests are the *Strong Vocational Interest Blank* and the *Kuder Preference Record-Occupational* (both of which are described later in this chapter), though these instruments seldom are used below the level of the senior high school.

Learning about the High School Program

Finding out what high school is like is also an important part of a guidance program. The high school principal or counselor visits the junior high school to tell students what the first year of high school will be like. Sometimes high school students one year older are brought back to relate their own experiences and impressions. Arrangements are made for the eighth-graders to visit the high school in groups and ask questions. Occasionally a high school will prepare a "Freshman Handbook" telling about the school, which is distributed to the prospective new students in the spring.

Learning about Jobs in Junior High School

The third important aspect of guidance in the junior high school is that of introducing the student to the world of work. This is not the age at which many schools encourage choice of vocational goals, but it is a time when they encourage young people to begin finding out what various kinds of jobs are like, what it takes in the way of training to get and hold them, what kinds of people enjoy them, and where they lead. This often starts as early as the sixth grade, when classes go to visit local industries and professional offices. It continues all through the junior high school years and on into the senior high school, usually at the rate and in the directions dictated by each student's individual curiosity or interest, but occasionally spurred by an arbitrary requirement by the school, such as: "Write on your ninth-grade registration form your first three present choices of vocational field." Students are always, however, encouraged to think of their choices as tentative, subject to later confirmation or revision as they learn more about vocations and about themselves.

At this age the goal is to get students to find out about jobs, rather than make judgments about them. There are increasing numbers of excellent reference materials pertaining to jobs, pamphlets written in language junior high school children can understand and arranged to provide a balanced and realistic picture of what it is like to work in a certain kind of job or profession. The point in all this is to permit even the first and most tentative choices of occupational goals to be informed choices. The boy who has done his best to avoid math and science, and has every intention of continuing to do so, should know at this point that if he wants to be a doctor he is going to have to star in science—and gleam at least a little in mathematics—even to get into the training for medicine. And he is much more likely to accept these hard facts of life—and surmount or adjust to them—if he finds them out himself than if he is simply told by some adult that they exist.

Since the point of entry into high school—at least, entry into tenth grade—often is the point at which young people are forced into their first either-or choice of educational patterns, and since some of these choices are becoming more difficult to modify or reverse, the focus of school guidance has moved downward on the ladder of grades. As early as the sixth grade in some schools, and in most schools no later than the ninth, every student must pull together all his information, consult his judgment, and choose his high school courses. If all his information leads him to look forward to continuation of school at a selective college, his choice should be that of four years of English, three or four years of mathematics, at least a year of science and two of social studies, and usually two years of one foreign language. This he should know before he fills his program with other courses. If all his information leads him to believe that he should leave school and look for work as soon as he reaches the legal age—a conclusion which the counselor will find hard to agree with—his choice should be that of general math and applied science rather than that of first-year algebra and biology. And if all his information leads to no final conclusions at all, as is the case with a majority of youngsters at this age, he will want to choose high school courses in a way that will keep open for him just as many doors as are realistically possible, for later decision.

In the period of choices encompassed by the junior high school years, then, tests and test scores—though only a part of all the information considered—have high value and frequent use in the process by which the student finds out about himself in the academic environment. His "fit" in the special life that is school is described about as well by test scores as by teachers' marks, but from a slightly more objective angle. And his assessment of his interests is both stimulated and guided by the interest inventories that the school lets him take—instruments that look like tests but work as guides for self-study. In finding out about the high school, and in the first explorations of what adult jobs are like, still other resources are used.

Testing in Guidance at the Senior High School Level

The sharp break that once existed between elementary school and high school, the traditional "everybody-out" shift from eighth grade to ninth and a kind of starting all over with a new set of teachers in a different building, is disappearing rapidly. Large proportions of school systems have filled in the break by inserting a junior high school between sixth and tenth grades. And even those systems which retain the 8–4 organization have built bridges of communication and guidance across the old gap, so that no longer are many high schools separated in the educational culture from the schools that send them students. One of the symptoms of the fusion of high schools and lower schools into one continuous system of education is the common salary scale, by which teachers of equal training and experience are paid at the same rate whether they teach a fourth-grade class or senior civics. And, in more and more school systems, information about students is being passed across the ancient crevasse.

This means that the guidance done in high schools usually represents a continuation of guidance rendered in earlier years. Thus, even though this description of guidance is broken into discrete intervals for the sake of discussion, guidance at the senior high school level in most schools simply picks up where junior high school guidance leaves off, and proceeds without missing a beat. The what-am-I-like question is extended and broadened, the what-is-school-like question is given some new kinds of attention, and the question of vocational choice is brought more nearly into focus.

To arm the student and his teachers and counselors with more, and more specific, information on the academic side of the what-am-I-like question, there is further formal testing in the high school. The student at this age is coming upon some real points of decision, and the additional tests have greater variety of both content and purpose.

In Minnesota, the state-wide testing program takes hold at the tenth grade. Students are given clear and objective information about where they stand among their age-mates from all over the state in certain kinds of academic learning. By testing this way as early as the ninth or tenth grade, it is possible to remind some youngsters that if they hope to hold to the career or educational goals they have set for themselves they will have to dig in a little harder. It is possible to suggest to some able students that they have set their sights on educational or career goals that are too low. And by this testing it is possible for educators in colleges as well as those in the high schools to identify, while there is still time to do something about it, the boys and girls whose academic learning rates indicate noteworthy promise. In the savings of "national resources in human talent," these wide-scale programs in the early high school years have immense value. And the central purpose of the testing programs at this level is guidance—in its best sense. It is testing to inform the student and to help him make better decisions, rather than to direct him.

Some subject matter tests are also given for teaching purposes in high school and, depending upon the practices of the school, they may have guidance uses as well as teaching uses. The tests given before, during, and at the end of a student's course in advanced algebra, for example, can be used to add to his fund of information about himself and his skills. What does it mean to him to be at the top—or at the bottom—of a "fast" section in geometry? How can he use the knowledge that he is the very best (by test) in the whole school in physics? If the results of tests used for teaching purposes are shared also with the guidance office and entered into the student's record for him to study and reflect on, there is an addition to his knowledge of himself that comes as a by-product of teaching.

Then there are some new kinds of tests, used primarily for guidance purposes. These are the aptitude tests. They are distinguished from the academic aptitude tests, or learning ability tests, that have been used all through the grades up to this point only because they attempt to measure certain kinds of developed ability in addition to those which are strictly academic. The section titles of a widely used test battery of this kind, the *Differential Aptitude Tests* (always referred to as the DAT) will illustrate the point. The subtests of the DAT are:

1. Verbal reasoning (30 minutes). Relationships among concepts stated in words—an academic task like that in academic ability tests.
2. Numerical ability (30 minutes). Mathematical skill in computation and reasoning—again an academic job just like those in academic ability tests.
3. Abstract reasoning (25 minutes). Understanding and applying ideas expressed in nonverbal, nonpictorial diagrams—the kind of puzzle job that appears in some academic ability tests.
4. Space relations (30 minutes). Visualizing solids and structural shapes from printed diagrams—a kind of test job that appears in some academic ability tests and seems to relate to the kinds of skills used in mechanical drawing.
5. Mechanical reasoning (30 minutes). Understanding and applying simple physical laws and forces to problems presented in pictures and diagrams—a kind of test job that does not appear in academic ability tests and that apparently is related to growing insights into things mechanical.
6. Clerical speed and accuracy (6 minutes). Speed and accuracy in perceiving and marking letter and number symbols—again, a test job that is not found in tests of academic ability, one that is related to some of the skills important in office work.
7. Spelling (10 minutes in *Language Usage Test*). A test job that appears in achievement tests at the lower grade levels, but not in tests of academic ability.
8. Sentences (25 minutes in *Language Usage Test*). Sensitivity to correctness of expression, punctuation, and word usage—again, a test job that appears often in achievement tests but not in academic ability tests.

In the DAT, obviously, there have been added some new dimensions to the testing of learning ability. In addition to the kinds of test jobs that appear in the strictly academic tests of ability (tests 1, 2, and 3), there are two long tests of developed abilities that relate to success in mechanical occupations (tests 4 and 5) and three tests to demonstrate skills useful in stenography and office jobs (tests 6, 7, and 8). The DAT is a guidance tool rather than a teaching or selection instrument and as such is used in thousands of high schools to help give young people some insights into the ways their skills are developing. DAT scores never tell a student that he should be anything, only that among his own academic and certain occupational skills there are some that seem to be more highly developed than others, and that among a large group of other students of his age these skills have given rankings. Among the tests now widely used for guidance with high school students, the *Differential Aptitude Tests* probably provide the greatest amount of useful and accurate what-am-I-like information for the greatest number of students. And, as is true of all tests (whether the covers say so or not), the DAT contains jobs on which the student demonstrates his learned skills—not psychological peeks into his innate but as yet undiscovered and undeveloped capacities.

There are available for use in the high school, too, a great many "aptitude" tests purporting to relate to the specialized abilities of certain vocations. There are tests of clerical aptitude that are measures of certain clerical skills already developed, tool-dexterity tests that are measures of manual proficiency already developed, mechanical aptitude tests measuring mechanical information, tests of musical talent and art judgment, tests of color blindness and color discrimination. The list is both long and interesting. The counselor in almost every high school has an assortment of them ready for use with students who express an interest in finding out more about themselves in the particular skills the tests measure.

It should always be pointed out to the fond parent, however, that none of these tests will tell a boy or girl whether or not he should try to be a musician or a mechanic or an atomic physicist. All it will do is permit the student to compare his already-developed skill in an area with the skills of other students like him. The judgment about what he should become, the choice of courses and careers, remains his. But most of the various aptitude tests, taken and interpreted in a sensible way, will add to the student's fund of knowledge about himself, which is the main purpose of guidance.

For students whose vocational interests lead them to seek tests beyond the range of instruments maintained by the school's guidance staff, there is still another source of aid. In most states, the state employment office or bureau maintains field offices in which it is possible for students to take the tests of vocational skill built by the United States Employment Service. These tests, and there are hundreds of them, have been built to assess some of the skills used in a whole variety of skilled and semiskilled occupations. A student with a serious interest in exploring his own skills in relation to those needed for a job as a plumber, for example, can through his counselor obtain an appointment at the employment office and take the appropriate tests.

Sometimes, students do not know where to turn for competent guidance testing if there is no guidance specialist in their own school. Guidance testing is done by a variety of public and private agencies, some very capable and some of doubtful competence. As a general rule for the student who seeks guidance testing outside his school, it is wise to call or write to the nearest state university—student counseling office or bureau—and ask for advice. Most state universities and many private colleges maintain excellent testing and counseling centers that are available to nonstudents. At the very least, the university's counseling office will be able to suggest other agencies where competent guidance testing may be obtained at modest cost. One additional source of helpful information is *A Guide to Guidance Resources,* available from the Evaluation and Advisory Service of Educational Testing Service, Princeton, New Jersey.

Interest Inventories as Counseling Aids in High Schools

It is at the high school level that the vocational interest inventories have their widest use and application. Several are available to schools, but two dominate the field: the *Strong Vocational Interest Blank* and the *Kuder Preference Record–Occupational.* These two are so widely used that their characteristics, and their differences, merit some description.

The *Strong* offers separate forms for men and women. In each case, it asks almost endless questions about what the student likes and dislikes in activities, studies, sports, reading, music, entertainment, conversation, company, and so on. There are nearly fifty occupational comparison groups for men—nearly thirty for women—as the student finds out when he gets his "profile" back. According to the way he has responded to the questions, his interests are interpreted as resembling the interests of people in certain occupations and not resembling interests of persons in other occupations. Then the student is told that his responses have been similar (or not similar) to those of a group of adults in a given occupation. For example: "The interests you expressed by your responses on this instrument are in general similar to the responses of adults who are successful accountants, auditors, bankers, and pharmacists." Used cautiously, the *Strong* helps a youngster to begin to locate himself in the adult world in terms of some of the things that are interesting and important to him. To know that his range and focus of interests correspond with those of successful adults in stated fields of work may suggest vocational possibilities not previously considered.

On the other hand, if he has been thinking that he wants to be a lawyer, but learns that the kinds of things that are particularly interesting to him are of little or no interest to lawyers already in practice, he would do well to reconsider whether he should persist in his intent to be a lawyer—although this may indeed be an excellent choice for him to make with his eyes open. The information obtained from the *Strong* test, therefore, may stimulate thinking about new interests and may confirm or cast doubt on already recognized interests. The scores obtained on the *Strong* inventory are not regarded as fixed pictures of any student's interests. The *Strong* profile says, "This is the way your responses compare with the responses of some adults who have been in these occupations for several years." And for this reason, the *Strong* often is administered a second time in college and in counseling centers for young people out of school.

The *Strong Vocational Interest Blank* deserves one additional comment here. It is an exceptionally useful tool in helping young people to know themselves better—but it is also one of the most widely misused instruments in the educational field. All too many counselors have permitted students and their parents to believe that scores on the *Strong* indicate that the student should be a lawyer or a farmer or a biologist or a store manager. Nothing in the whole field of guidance activity is as wrong or as dangerous as this interpretation. The *Strong* inventory pertains only to personal interests and has no bearing whatever on the skills and training required for occupations. Whenever a student says to his parents, "I took a vocational interest inventory and it says I should be . . . ," somebody has erred badly.

The other widely used inventory of interests, the *Kuder Preference*

Record, comes in two different packages. One explores student interests in relation to sixty-one specific jobs—farmer, forester, county agent, minister, and so on—and is entitled *Kuder Preference Record–Occupational.* The other explores student interests as they pertain to ten general kinds of vocational activity—mechanical, computational, scientific, literary, persuasive, artistic, musical, social service, clerical, "outdoor"—and is called *Kuder Preference Record–Vocational.* This makes for some confusion among the uninitiated, for one must always be sure which *Kuder* has been used when the results are discussed. The discussion here pertains to the *Occupational* scale, which is the more recent form of the inventory.

The *Kuder* inventory is used for the same purposes, and in the same general ways, as the *Strong* inventory. It takes less time to give and to score than the *Strong,* and thus has some practical advantages in the school; but it has not yet been researched as intensively nor with as many occupational groups; so the *Strong* is still regarded as the "senior instrument" by professionals. The *Kuder* is different from the *Strong* in one subtle but very important way that often is overlooked by counselors. The interests assessed in the *Strong* inventory are all interests held by adults—music, art, religion, hobbies, sports, entertainment, as well as interests in work activities. The *Kuder,* on the other hand, samples only interests that are related directly to the kinds of things adults do in their work. In effect, then, the *Strong* tries to answer the question "In what kinds of work are the successful people who have interests like mine?" while in general the *Kuder* tries to answer the question "In what kinds of jobs will the work most nearly match my present interests?"

Although both the *Strong* and the *Kuder* inventories are designed for appropriate use with high school students, a preponderance of practice has seen the *Kuder* used more often with younger students, in junior high school and early high school years, and the *Strong* used more often with senior high school students and college freshmen.

Personality Tests as Counseling Aids in High Schools

There is another kind of inventory that must be covered in this listing, though it is more talked about than used. This is the "personality test" or "personal inventory" or "scale of personal characteristics"—a category of instruments which custom permits us to call simply "personality tests." By actual count in the most recent bibliography of tests in print, there are 135 tests of personality characteristics available for use in high schools by counselors or school psychologists, not counting about an equal number that are designed for research use only or for clinical use with institutionalized patients. The characteristics they aim to measure range from mental health to social adjustment to ego strength to self-reliance—and beyond.

Measurement of personal qualities has not yet reached the level of validity and reliability needed to make it both safe and helpful in school use. Many of the instruments in the personality test category are highly respectable tools in the hands of clinical psychologists or psychiatrists; others are useful tools of research by experimental psychologists; still others are toe-holds on the edge of personality measurement and are published only so that other researchers can use them and improve on them. Most of them are the products of long effort by able and dedicated professionals. Some of them are perfectly innocuous in their practical usefulness; others are about as safe for general use as a do-it-yourself atomic energy kit. For the present then, the measurement of human personality characteristics is in the laboratory stage of development and not yet ready for general school use.

But perhaps this qualification needs qualification. The counselors and psychologists in schools often are themselves researchers, formally or informally. Or they may be working with researchers. In either case, they may have very laudable reasons for administering certain personality tests to students in the school; the reasons always have to do with the search for a better way somehow to observe and assess personality characteristics in young people. Very often such a researcher in the school will obtain permission from the students and parents to administer an experimental instrument and will describe its content and purpose. Almost always the researcher will obtain prior permission from administrators and school board. Such research among school students is necessary if better techniques are to be found, just as the vaccines for polio protection had to be tried on hundreds of thousands of people before one was found that was both effective and safe. For these good reasons, the use of personality tests should not be barred altogether from the schools, but should be permitted in ways and at times that serve legitimate research purposes. It goes almost without saying, however, that even in its research applications a test of personality factors should not violate good taste, should never hang tags or labels on a youngster that describe him in ways he cannot understand or that can be used to affect his life.

There are some instruments in the personality domain that appear to be coming close to levels of validity, reliability, and safety that general school use demands; so the time will come when the general warning against personality measures can be lifted—a time perhaps not far off.

Guidance Testing and College Admissions Testing

Guidance testing is, of course, closely related to testing for college admissions. Educational practices in this country are so wonderfully varied that in some places (like Minnesota) the tests designed principally for guidance of young people in high school have by-product uses for admission to college, and in other places (like Georgia) the tests designed principally for admission to college have by-product uses in high school guidance. And in Michigan the guidance *is* the admission to college, at least to the university. So one can start the discussion at either end, or in the middle.

In some communities—too many, really—parental and social pressures for "choice of college" begin to build up as early as the eighth grade. That is, in these particular subcultures, going to the "right" college or group of colleges is so important to parents that they begin to inquire while the child is still in elementary school, "Will he be admitted to Old Ivy, or should I put him into a special prep school?" More to protect and help the student than to assure the anxious parent, the counselor seeks some clues for long-range prediction. There are some such clues now, and their number will increase.

In one study, students tested in all grades from eighth through twelfth with the *School and College Ability Test* were kept track of until they had taken the College Board's *Scholastic Aptitude Test*. From the SCAT score records these youngsters earned, as early as the eighth grade, the publisher of SCAT was able to develop charts for the prediction of the College Board scores the students would be likely to earn. Since the SCAT instruments have verbal and quantitative scores resembling the SAT scores, and content that is roughly the same, the "bridge" from early SCAT scores to twelfth-grade SAT scores is not quite as rickety as it would be if some other type of academic ability test were used as the predictor. The counselor also has other references which tell him the ranges of SAT scores currently found acceptable by various institutions. So the counselor looks up a given student's SCAT scores, earned two months before, and sits down with the charts shown in Figure 10. Taking the student's SCAT verbal score (SCAT-V) of 288, earned in the eighth grade, he can go upward in the column to where he finds it on the chart and estimate the chances of the student's earning a given SAT verbal score when he reaches College Board age in the twelfth grade. The college of his choice currently is accepting applicants half of whom have SAT verbal scores of 550 and higher; so the counselor looks at the intersection of the student's eighth-grade SCAT scores with the curved line that represents an SAT-V score of 550 and is able to say to him and his parents, "If his academic growth for the next four years follows a pattern like that of the students used in the prediction study—and if the college's admissions policies remain about the same—the odds will be about 70 out of 100 that he will earn an SAT verbal score just about at the average for admitted students."

Prediction of this kind, from test to test, works in the other direction, too. If the student and his parents have too early developed college hopes that are likely to be unrealistic—that is, if the college he is thinking about is very highly selective on criteria of academic skill and admits only students with extremely high test scores and grade averages, and he has all along been just a good C-plus student with undistinguished test performances—the counselor will be doing them all a real guidance service if he uses the prediction data to help them realize that this individual's chances of entering the chosen college are likely to be very slim indeed. There are realities in the academic world that can be ignored only so long; admission to a selective college is one of them. If a counselor can use test-to-test predictions to warn students of these realities, to motivate them to greater effort, and at the same time work out with them some alternate choices that may be more realistic, the test information will have been used for good guidance.

And there is still another way that early predictions are used. There

FIGURE 10. *Predicting College Board SAT Scores from Earlier Scores Earned on SCAT*

Chances in 100 That Students with Various Scores on SCAT Verbal Will Earn Selected Scores on SAT Verbal

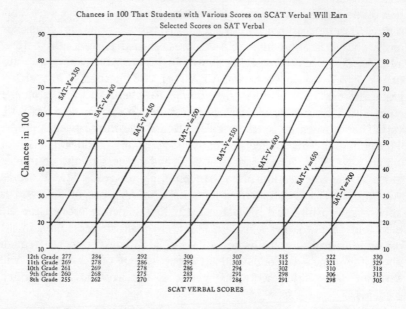

	12th Grade	11th Grade	10th Grade	9th Grade	8th Grade
	277	269	261	260	255
	284	278	269	268	262
	292	286	278	275	270
	300	295	286	283	277
	307	303	294	291	284
	315	312	302	298	291
	322	321	310	306	298
	330	329	318	313	305

SCAT VERBAL SCORES

Chances in 100 That Students with Various Scores on SCAT Quantitative Will Earn Selected Scores on SAT Mathematics

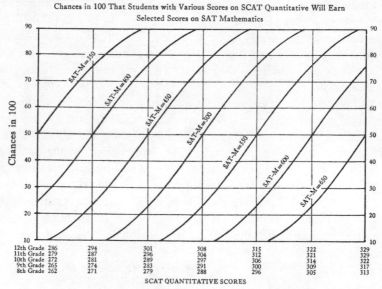

	12th Grade	11th Grade	10th Grade	9th Grade	8th Grade
	286	279	272	265	262
	294	287	281	274	271
	301	296	289	283	279
	308	304	297	291	288
	315	312	306	300	296
	322	321	314	309	305
	329	329	322	317	313

SCAT QUANTITATIVE SCORES

are students in the upper grades and junior high school who are brilliant academically but have neither hopes nor plans for continuing their education beyond the high school. Usually such students come from families in which going to college has not been the habit or expectation, where even the notion of having a child go on to college is received with some hostility. Culture changes of the last two decades have done much to reduce such hostile reaction to the idea of college-going, but there remains a fairly large segment of the population in which the prospect of college is so unfamiliar that parents and children have a "Who-me?" attitude when the suggestion is made that a youngster among them ought to go to college. Test scores that predict college abilities before students are completely committed to high school programs that will bar them from college are used both to find and to convince students whose abilities far exceed their educational plans. As an example, take the case of Joan, a fourteen-year-old who had an IQ of 131 on the *Otis Beta,* and 134 on the *Lorge-Thorndike.* On the *Iowa Tests of Basic Skills,* her composite percentile rank was 96. Joan's teacher wrote this report: "When Joan began planning for the tenth grade, she asked to be changed from the academic to the commercial course. She said her parents did not believe in college training for girls. A parent conference revealed the family's conviction that their financial condition put college out of Joan's reach. After we pointed out her test scores and her potential, her parents agreed that Joan's chances for success should not be hampered. We discussed ways by which scholarship funds and our job placement facilities could help Joan get a college education. The scores of the standardized tests convinced Joan's parents of her ability far more than did her report cards, although she had made an average above 90 all during junior high school." This, too, is the kind of guidance that counts in the utilization of human talent, especially when it can be accomplished early.

The "bridge" just described, from SCAT to SAT, is not by any means the only test-to-test prediction used in high school guidance. The *Differential Aptitude Tests,* described earlier in this chapter, have also been linked to the SAT in long-range predictions. In Florida, there is a state-wide program by which every student is tested in the ninth grade; scores predict quite well how each student is likely to do—unless he changes dramatically in both interest and drive—on the state-wide tests which are given in the twelfth grade for admission to the state universities. A number of high school counselors have built their own bridges of prediction data, from tests used in their schools, by following up students as they mature and comparing their later test scores or college admissions experiences with their early test scores. The whole business of prediction amounts to no more than a calculation of odds on the basis of experience and performance.

As students grow older and progress upward in the high school grades, their what-am-I-like questions are mixed more and more with what-should-I-do-next questions or, more accurately, the question "What choices are open to me now?" When the choices to be considered are those of where to go to college, test data for guidance abound. In the fall of the junior year, students who want to explore college possibilities take the *Preliminary Scholastic Aptitude Test,* described in Chapter 7. This test is directly related to the College Board SAT and predicts SAT scores from only a year away. On it, a student's performance as a junior predicts his senior performance on the SAT about as accurately as if his junior test were the SAT itself. Since the PSAT is designed for guidance use, it provides a whole variety of information for interpretation and can be used with the "profiles" of colleges in terms of scores earned by accepted freshmen. The story of Fred in Chapter 7 illustrates how the PSAT is used.

The University System of Georgia has developed for high school counselors in the state one of the most sophisticated and useful techniques known for the guidance use of test scores. Description of the Georgia technique will afford illustration of the kinds of test use that all counselors strive for. In Georgia, all eight institutions in the State University System require applicants to submit scores on the College Board *Scholastic Aptitude Test* to be considered for admission, as do twenty other colleges not associated with the University System. This common test requirement makes the SAT scores a sort of common currency in the state, and affords some real advantages. By keeping track of students' SAT scores, average high school grades, and grades earned in Georgia colleges—over a period of several years—the Office of Testing and Guidance was able to put together an experience table for every college but one in the state.

Each experience table contains a formula representing the combination of high school grade average and SAT test scores that is most predictive of success in the freshman year of the particular named college, and provides a table of odds favoring the earning of each passing grade. The combination of test scores and high school averages that is most predictive of success is different at almost every college and, of course, the odds for earning a B or an A are at least slightly different at every college. The high school average (HSA) is the arithmetic mean (average) of high school grades, where each A has a value of 40; B, a value of 30; C, a value of 20; D, a value of 10; and F is counted in with a value of 0. Hence, an HSA of 25 is midway between a C and a B. Using Figure 11, try a sample:

A senior boy in a Georgia high school with a high school average of B (30), an SAT verbal score of 500, and an SAT mathematical score of 400 would like to go to a private college. To find how he might be expected to do at Oglethorpe University, he goes to the table for Oglethorpe University and converts the information about himself into that special index. The formula for the index at Oglethorpe is the SAT verbal score plus 20 times the high school average (V + 20 HSA)—in this hypothetical case, 500 + 600, or 1,100. In the list of index numbers he sees that his odds for earning a C or better the first year are about 70 out of 100; his odds for earning a B or better are only about 10 out of 100, and the odds in favor of earning an A average are practically nil. Trying another table out of curiosity, he finds that his odds for earning a C average at Berry College are 68 out of 100.

No one, of course, can predict accurately what a particular student will do when he gets to college, because so very many factors are involved. But on the basis of what other students with similar scores and grade averages have done in the past, one can say: "Out of 100 males with an index just the same as his who have enrolled in Oglethorpe University, 70 earned average grades of C or better in the freshman year, 10 earned B or better, and none earned A averages." Any one individual, for a variety of reasons, may do better or worse than the average.

Look for a moment at the table for Emory at Oxford to see how the same senior boy might fare at that college. In this index, you use his mathematical score rather than his verbal score on the SAT.

Figure 11. *Using High School Grades and SAT Scores to Predict Success in Georgia Colleges**

Proportions of Students with Various Index Scores (Based on Formulas Using College Board Scores and High School Average) Who Will Make An Average College Grade of C or Better, B or Better, and A Their First Year

BERRY COLLEGE

Males   *N = 141*

INDEX	STUDENT WILL GET AVERAGE OF:		
V + 26 HSA	C	B	A
1900	.99	.71	.14
1800	.97	.60	.08
1700	.95	.50	.05
1600	.91	.39	.03
1500	.86	.29	.01
1400	.79	.20	
1300	.70	.13	
1200	.60	.08	
1100	.49	.05	
1000	.38	.03	
900	.28	.01	
800	.20		
700	.13		
600	.08		
500	.05		
400	.03		
300	.01		

COLUMBUS COLLEGE

Males   *N = 104*

INDEX	STUDENT WILL GET AVERAGE OF:		
V + 11 HSA	C	B	A
1300	.99	.97	.51
1200	.97	.90	.27
1100	.89	.74	.11
1000	.73	.50	.03
900	.49	.26	.01
800	.25	.10	
700	.10	.03	
600	.03	.01	
500	.01		
400			
300			

EMORY AT OXFORD

Males — N = 91

INDEX M + 18 HSA	STUDENT WILL GET AVERAGE OF:		
	C	B	A
1600	.99	.77	.13
1500	.96	.63	.06
1400	.91	.47	.03
1300	.83	.31	.01
1200	.71	.18	
1100	.55	.09	
1000	.39	.04	
900	.24	.02	
800	.13		
700	.06		
600	.03		
500	.01		
400			

OGLETHORPE UNIVERSITY

Males — N = 60

INDEX V + 20 HSA	STUDENT WILL GET AVERAGE OF:		
	C	B	A
1700		.90	.29
1600	.99	.80	.17
1500	.96	.66	.08
1400	.92	.50	.03
1300	.83	.33	.01
1200	.70	.19	
1100	.54	.10	
1000	.37	.04	
900	.23	.02	
800	.12	.01	
700	.05		
600	.02		
500	.01		
400			

SOURCE: Reproduced with permission from "Supplement to the Counselor's Guide to Georgia Colleges," by John R. Hills, Pauline B. Masters, and Linda B. Emory. Office of Testing and Guidance, Regents of the University System of Georgia, Atlanta 3, Georgia.

* This table is reproduced for illustrative purposes only. Since the data are subject to periodic revisions, the table is not usable for current predictions by readers of this book.

Mathematical (400) plus 18 times HSA (30) equals an index of 940. Reading across the table between the lines of 900 and 1,000 (interpolating) you see that his odds for a C average are about 45 out of 100, for a B only three out of 100, and for an A, nil.

With tables like these for every college in the state but one, including tables for the major divisions within the larger universities, the Georgia student and his counselor can find out what the student's chances of success will be before the student has to make his choice. How much better this is than to tell a student that he is not "college material"—or to send him off to a college where failure falls upon him without warning.

When tests are given in ways and at times that add to the student's information about himself, then, they are effective guidance tools in the high school. So are tests that add to his insights into experiences that lie ahead of him: What is college like? What are jobs like? What are the people like who work at the jobs I'm thinking about? Where do I fit into all these things? How do I stack up in comparison with these older groups of people? What are my best choices? By providing some cold-blooded and impersonal comparative information on these points, wisely used tests strengthen and improve the choices made by young people, at a time when they have many important choices to make.

Testing in Guidance at the College Level

The gap between high school and college is almost as wide and deep as it was a generation ago. There are movements afoot to bridge this gap, but it is still generally true that some colleges act as if their new freshmen had been born at the age of eighteen, the day before they showed up on the campus. For this reason, students in most colleges start off with clean slates, bare records, a new chance—and their counselors begin collecting information about them all over again.

Because the high school records that are forwarded to colleges usually report scores on tests in ways that make college interpretation difficult, the college student finds himself taking again many of the tests he has already taken in high school. Probably the forms of the tests are different; so he does not encounter the same questions; but the tests and interpretations are the same. Not all of the tests he takes in this rash of examinations will be repeats of tests he took in high school, of course. Some of them will be subject matter tests for placement in courses, and several of them will have been built by departments of the college.

After his tests are scored, the student sits down with that member of the faculty who has been designated as his adviser and who has temporary possession of all the college's information about the student—interview records, such high school records as the college may have obtained, notes of recommendation, and the test scores. The quality and realism of the counseling he receives during this one-hour period depend almost wholly on the interest and technical skill of the faculty adviser. If the adviser is one who takes this annual assignment seriously, who accepts test information for what it is and has learned how to use it well, who considers all of the pertinent information available on the student, and who thinks the advising of freshmen is as important to the college as the counseling of majors in his field, the guidance which the new student receives in this interview is likely to be extremely good. If the adviser is doing this job while protesting the indignity under his breath, however, or if he discounts tests altogether and prefers to trust only his perceptions of the student in the interview, the student would be better off to make his own choice of courses on the basis of what he knows about himself.

Once past the whirl and quick decisions of Freshman Week, any college student may visit the guidance office. Some of the visits come about as a consequence of his own questions and need for help, others because such visits are scheduled regularly by the college, others because the dean has sent an urgent and pointed request. For whatever reasons he makes these visits, the student and his counselors build up a record of information about him, a record consisting of course grades, interview data, and test scores. The general purpose and procedure are exactly the same as they were in high school guidance: to increase the student's understanding of himself, of his present environment, and of the opportunities that are open to him. Even though the high school record that has followed him to college may be sparse, he remembers the generalizations he had made about himself earlier and reinforces or revises them in the light of his growing ability to assess himself. Supporting and strengthening these more mature assessments of himself are his performances on tests—tests of academic skill, tests of subject learning, inventories of interests. To the student, these tests represent trials of skill, demonstrations of strength in the new and more competitive environment that college affords. He uses tests to flex some intellectual muscles that he did not know he had. Sometimes he asks to take certain tests a second time, after a period of hard work, to see for himself what changes he has wrought.

A good guidance center in a college or university is an active, interesting place. It is directed by a professional person who has had specific training in college guidance work and who, in most colleges, has full faculty status. Usually there are one or more younger professionals assisting the director and sharing the counseling load. There are rooms for private interviews, rooms for administering tests to small groups, and places where individuals can take tests alone. In all this, whether the guidance office is large or small, the student senses at once that he is the focus of attention. This place and these people are here to help him find out more about himself.

In many colleges, there is a standard program of testing that is administered to all students at stated times: the placement testing of arriving freshmen, perhaps a battery of general achievement tests in major learning areas at the end of the freshman year, another battery of general achievement tests at the end of the sophomore year, some special subject achievement tests at that point in time when sophomores must demonstrate their readiness for major concentrations in the junior year. But the guidance testing in college differs most from the guidance testing in high school in the amount of individual or non-scheduled testing that is done. Partly because there is more counselor time per student enrolled, and, usually, more adequate facilities, and partly because the more mature students seek out test experiences, there is a great deal more of individual test-taking to pursue individual student inquiries.

So the testing for guidance in the early years of college both overlaps and extends the testing done for the same purpose in high schools. With formal and fully validated tests, it gives the student more opportunities to try himself out on the kinds of work that schooling demands, to compare himself with his peers in a competitive world.

Testing for guidance goes on, of course, not only in the upper reaches of higher education, but also in centers for adult education and in private counseling enterprises. Its principal characteristics are the same at all levels and in all places—the test is a trial job and the score is a comparison of performances. Next to the application of testing to the function of teaching, the uses of measurement in guidance are the most fruitful ones in education.

CHAPTER 9

HELPING STUDENTS
TO DO THEIR BEST

Living comfortably with tests, taking them in stride and doing as well as you possibly can on them without the tensions that waste energy, requires a certain basic knowledge of what tests are like. Earlier chapters in this book have covered that basic knowledge in considerable depth, but a quick summary will be offered here.

For comfort in the face of an approaching test, nothing beats "knowing your stuff," and knowing that you know it. No amount of "test-wiseness" or inside information or last-minute cramming is a substitute for clear command of the skills and knowledge to be demonstrated on the test—either for the sake of calmness before the test or for the sake of a good score report after it. So the things to know and do listed here are to be considered additional provisions for test comfort after the student has done all he can to develop the learnings which the test will ask him to demonstrate.

Finding Out What an Important Test Is Like Ahead of Time

Students should be told ahead of time that an important standardized test is coming. Drawing on materials provided by the publisher, the school should inform students about the nature of the tests. The explanation should include the length of time of each test, generally the topics or skills it will cover, whether students are expected to finish the test (speed or power test), whether or not there is a penalty for guessing when one is not sure of the answer, what forms the answers will take—multiple-choice, short answer, or other—and what past tests students have taken that this new one may resemble.

Whether the information is provided routinely by teachers and counselors or ferreted out by the student himself in asking questions, here are the things he ought to know about the nature and ground rules of a test before the day he takes it:

1. What will it cover? If it is to be a test of academic ability, what skills others than the verbal and quantitative ones will be measured, if any? If it is an English test, what proportions of it are devoted to rules of grammar, spelling, usage, reading comprehension, literature? If it is a history test, what historical period will it cover? If it is a mathematics test, what concepts and topics will it cover? Without yielding specific test information, it is both fair and sensible to let the students know what kind of a job the test will present. It is not a part of testing to "surprise" the examinee when the purpose of testing is to assess his learning.

2. How long will it be? Most people unconsciously pace themselves to the expected length of a task, and knowing well ahead of time that a test battery is going to take four one-hour sessions rather than one thirty-five-minute sitting is important.

3. Will there be a penalty for wrong answers? Unless penalties for guessing—or the lack of them—are clearly spelled out, some students will not put down an answer unless they are absolutely sure of it, while others (the gamblers) will guess wildly. To keep the test from becoming a measure of audacity which penalizes the timid ones, the procedure for scoring the test needs to be stated specifically and honestly—read from the directions for giving the test, if possible.

4. Has the student taken another form of this test, or another test like it, before? If it is a familiar test that is coming up, there may be less need to ask questions.

5. What are the test materials like? Will the individual have to manage a whole deskful of papers? Is there any tricky answer sheet in which holes must be punched or tabs lifted off? What will the mechanics of the job be?

6. What kind of answer sheet will be used? The advent of electric and electronic test-scoring equipment has made scoring quicker and

cheaper, but it has put upon the student a responsibility for using somewhat complicated coded forms for his identification and the notation of his answers. Unless a student has had experience in using a particular answer sheet, and has proved that he can use it without error, he should be given a chance to study it—preferably to practice using it—before he faces it in the testing room. Without advance information about a complicated answer sheet, the test will be for some students one in decoding and using answer sheets.

In some schools that use tests wisely, the students are given an opportunity ahead of time to try their hands at a couple of sample questions and to practice in marking the separate answer sheet if separate answer sheets are unfamiliar.

For most of the tests that have a bearing on important decisions in school, information is not hard to obtain. To help students get ready for its tests, the College Entrance Examination Board publishes a whole series of descriptive bulletins, practice exercises, and brochures. For another series of tests used more for teaching and guidance, there is a motion picture that prepares students for the tests. For still other tests there are materials for class sessions, describing the tests.

How to Prepare for a Standardized Test

People preparing to take a test are about as different in their approaches as ballplayers coming to bat. Some players spit on their hands, some pick up a handful of dirt, some carefully straighten their caps, some shift their chewing gum from right side to left, and some do all of these things. The list of suggestions that teachers—and parents—might make to students who are preparing for a test is not long, but all the suggestions are important.

1. It is sensible to review, if one has time before taking an achievement test, but not blindly. Any big test that comes along will cover learnings that have been acquired over a long time, so it will be too late to try to do all the original reading or practice that should have been done. A general review of the main ideas in a course or subject will help to refresh them in the individual's memory.

2. It is useless to cram the night before the test. Last-minute

burning of the midnight oil may save a student's scalp with a teacher-made test, but for a standardized test this is worse than no preparation. The standardized test is less devoted to factual information than to skill in using information, so a person's chances of acquiring needed facts in a last-minute cram session are next to nil. Not even professional coaching schools that claim to prepare students for college admissions tests can accomplish any significant changes by cramming. There is no late and short substitute for learning that should have been acquired over a long period of time—at least not in the academic subjects. To attempt it is to ask for other handicaps on the test—fatigue and confusion.

3. Having reviewed sensibly as much as possible in the time available, most students are better off to relax by doing something different to take their minds off the test the afternoon and evening before the test comes up. A good night's sleep is a good investment.

4. Most important of all, of course, is to encourage learning the things at the time and in the sequence in which the school teaches them. If a student has done this, when any test comes along he is prepared.

Hints on Taking a Standardized Test

Some students have a slight advantage over others in taking tests because they have acquired, through experience or study, a kind of test know-how. Much of this know-how applies to all standardized tests and resembles, in its application, the advantage an experienced taxpayer has in filling out the federal income tax return. The object is not to cheat, but to avoid unnecessary losses.

Much of what a student needs to do he can do before he encounters the test face to face. In the testing situation itself, there are things to be done just before the test starts or while it is being taken.

1. The student must be sure that he understands the directions. After he has read the directions aloud, the examiner will pause and ask the group if anyone has any questions. If any part of what is to be done is not crystal-clear, the student should raise his hand and ask the question. This is why the examiner paused to ask for questions. In an important test, it is sheer idiocy to start work before all the directions are clearly understood. And if there is confusion about

directions in the interior of the test, the examiner or proctor will come to the student's seat and help interpret the directions.

2. The identification blanks on the answer sheet must be filled out exactly as the examiner directs, while he is giving these directions. If the student is reading something else while these directions are given, intending to complete these blanks after he has finished the test, there is a chance that he will forget something important.

3. Digging in the way a sprinter does to start a race and being prepared to concentrate one's whole attention on the test for the whole time that is allowed may be hard for people who are not accustomed to concentrating on anything for more than ten minutes at a time, but it is worth practicing. Experienced examiners are accustomed to seeing students lose score points after about fifteen minutes because they cannot concentrate their attention any longer.

4. It is best to work first through all the questions or problems that one knows the answers to without hesitation or doubt. This is insurance that one will have an opportunity to try the tasks that are easy. If a question or problem is going to take some thought, come back to it later. This is the single most important know-how skill in taking tests. The painfully methodical person who cannot bear to leave a question unanswered before going to the next one is handicapped on a standardized test, especially if it is a speed test. On the other hand, flipping from question to question without giving each one a good try is unwise.

5. Students should be warned to read all the answer choices given for every question, even on the first pass and on the questions they know without hesitation. Making an answer choice without reading all the options is folly. The wrong answers among the options given often are the answers obtained by people who have not read the question accurately or completely. So, as insurance against the errors of hasty reading of the question, the student should never fail to read all the answer choices.

6. On the second pass, in coming back to the questions skipped on the first time over, the best way is to go at each question and its answer options like Sherlock Holmes—looking for clues. Eliminating the answer options you are pretty certain are wrong and then studying the remaining ones may reveal some forgotten clue in your head or in the question. If the student narrows the options down to two, he has

increased his odds for choosing the right answer from one in five to one in two. Usually, the correct answers to a lot of questions will become clear when this technique has been applied, and there will then be no need for guessing. Information will have been used to eliminate the wrong answers and deduce the correct one—a perfectly respectable procedure in all academic circles. If the student is still stumped after a reasonable time, it may be best to pass the question again and leave it for a third round. If time is short and he has narrowed his choices down to two or three, he should mark the one that on the whole seems most likely.

7. Procedure as to guessing should depend on what the directions have said about guessing. If the directions or the examiner have said specifically that a scoring penalty will be assessed for every wrong answer, it is unwise to guess at an answer unless the choices have been reduced to two or three. If the guess must be among more options in answer to a question, the odds are likely to be against the guesser. BUT, if the directions say nothing about a penalty for wrong answers, or if they say only to "avoid wild guessing," or if they say that the score will be the total of the correct answers, it is wise to put down an answer to every question.

8. If a student finishes all questions in the test before time is called, he should go back and study again the questions about which he had the most doubt. Here is a point at which too many students pass up an opportunity for gaining another score point or two. They heave a sigh of relief after completing the second pass; think, "That's the best I can do"; and quit. Almost always there is at least one question that can be answered, or answered better, given a little more attention.

9. You cannot fudge extra score points by leaving small pencil marks around on the machine-scorable answer sheet. There was a time when scoring machines did accumulate a few extra points from pencil marks concealed in printed matter on the answer sheet, but that time is long past. And the machine cannot be fooled if two answers are put down in the case of a doubtful choice. Scoring machines these days read every pencil mark on the sheet, however faint, and consider its meaning. If there are two answer marks for any question, real or accidental, the machine will either ignore both of them, recognize the darker mark, or subtract points for the

double-marked question, depending on the particular machine. Any such efforts to fool the machine will not work and will also waste valuable time.

When tests are taken as they are intended to be taken, as interesting job samples on which the student can try out his hard-won skills, the process is stimulating for most students and enjoyable for many. Learning is a satisfying experience; and as testing is the proving part of that experience, it, too, can be satisfying and enjoyable. More important than the satisfactions it gives directly to students, though, is the guidance that good testing gives to the teacher, the counselor, the admissions officer, and the student himself.

APPENDIX

"Multiple-Choice Questions:
A Close Look"

The Test Development Division of Educational Testing Service has recently published a pamphlet, "Multiple-Choice Questions: A Close Look." Parts of this pamphlet are reprinted in this appendix for the reader who may be interested in what is done with the multiple-choice form of question in many present-day tests.

As the introduction to the pamphlet states:

The purpose of this close look at a group of multiple-choice questions is to dispel a myth: the myth of the multiple-choice question as a superficial exercise — one that requires little thought, less insight, and no understanding. Like other myths, this one may be based on a shadowy memory of the past, but it bears little relation to present reality. "What is often overlooked . . . ," writes Jerome Bruner in *The Process of Education,* "is that examinations can also be allies in the battle to improve curricula and teaching. Whether an examination is of the 'objective' type involving multiple choices or of the essay type, it can be devised so as to emphasize an understanding of the broad principles of a subject. Indeed, even when one examines detailed knowledge, it can be done in such a way as to require understanding by the student of the connectedness between specific facts."

The questions which appear on the following pages have been taken from a variety of tests constructed by Educational Testing Service. Many similar questions are now in use. Those presented here are as they appeared in the original tests, with the directions, when given, as they were given to the students. Each question is followed by a statistical analysis of its performance and by a brief discussion of the thought processes involved in formulating the question and in arriving at the correct answer.

Study of this representative sample of multiple-choice questions should lead to a clearer understanding of their potentialities, and should help to dispel the myth that "objective" tests require no thought, insight, or understanding.

Index to Questions

Question 1

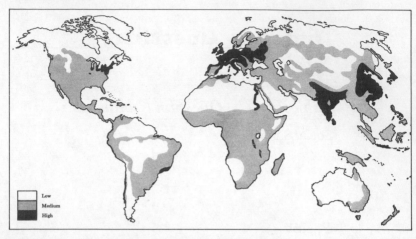

The shading on the above map is used to indicate

(A) population density
(B) percentage of total labor force in agriculture
(C) per capita income
(D) death rate per thousand of population

Statistical Analysis

RESPONSES	Students Classified by Total Test Score				
	LOWEST FIFTH	NEXT LOWEST FIFTH	MIDDLE FIFTH	NEXT HIGHEST FIFTH	HIGHEST FIFTH
Omit	1				
*A	45	52	53	58	58
B	6	1	2	1	1
C	6	5	1		1
D	2	2	4	1	
Total	60	60	60	60	60

Per cent of total group of 300 students answering correctly . . .   89%
Correlation between success on this question and total score on test .47

In many of the multiple-choice questions included in tests in the social sciences, an attempt is made to require the student to make use of his general background of knowledge in the interpretation of materials. Thus, this question does not simply ask: What areas of the world have the highest population densities? Rather, it presents a novel situation in which the

---

*Correct answer

student must infer that, of the choices offered, only population density provides a plausible explanation of the shadings on the map.

This question was answered correctly by almost 90 per cent of a group of college seniors. However, although large numbers of lower ability students were successful on it, the question did differentiate between some of the very poorest students and the rest of those tested.

An examination of the map clearly shows that choice (A), population density, is the proper response. The darkest shading, which according to the map's legend indicates the highest degree of whatever the shading represents, covers such high population density areas as the northeastern part of the United States, a large part of Europe, the Nile valley, India, Japan, and Eastern China. If this were not a sufficient clue, the areas with the lightest shading include such underpopulated areas as the Arctic regions, tropical South America, the Sahara and Arabian deserts, and most of Australia.

Choice (B), the percentage of total labor force in agriculture, while possibly attractive if only India and China are examined, is clearly incorrect when applied to the Northeastern United States. This choice was taken by 10 per cent of the least able group, but was not attractive to any of the other groups.

Choice (C), per capita income, attracted moderately those in the lowest two-fifths of the group. Per capita income could be plausible only if the student's analysis of the map took in solely the dark shading in the United States and Western Europe, and even there it is not entirely correct, but the dark shading in China and India could certainly not indicate high per capita income. The reverse observation is true of choice (D), death rate per thousand of population, since the latter might be expected to be high for India and China, but low for the United States and Europe. Only nine students selected this choice.

Question 2

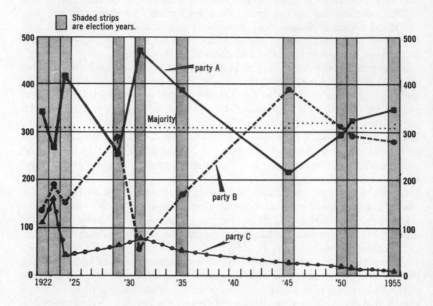

Shaded strips are election years.

The graph above represents the political composition from 1922 to 1955 of which of the following?

- (A) German Bundestag
- (B) French National Assembly
- (C) Italian Chamber of Deputies
- (D) British House of Commons

Statistical Analysis

RESPONSES	Students Classified by Total Test Score				
	LOWEST FIFTH	NEXT LOWEST FIFTH	MIDDLE FIFTH	NEXT HIGHEST FIFTH	HIGHEST FIFTH
Omit	8	1	3	2	
A	5	4	5	4	2
B	25	28	14	11	3
C	6	5	6	5	6
*D	16	22	32	38	49
Total	60	60	60	60	60

Per cent of total group of 300 students answering correctly . . . 52%
Correlation between success on this question and total score on test .49

---

*Correct answer

To answer this question correctly, the student must be able to do several things. First, he must be able to read the graph. Then, using the information he can infer from it, he must interpret it in the light of his knowledge of European history and government from 1922 to 1955 and draw a conclusion concerning which legislative body may properly be so depicted. In such a process, it is possible for different students to make use of different information to arrive at the correct answer.

In examining the graph, the student should note that the party system shown is essentially a two-party one, although there is a third party that, for most of the period shown, decreased in representation. He may also note the years in which elections were held, the years that Party A received majorities, the fact that Party B did not receive a majority until 1945, and the fact that in the elections of 1923 and 1929 neither party received a majority.

In considering the first of the four possible answers, the German Bundestag, the student should recognize that during the period through 1932, that of the Weimar Republic, no single party in Germany was able to attain a majority, partly because of the multiplicity of parties. After Hitler came to power in 1933, parties other than the Nazi Party were outlawed. These facts do not fit the graph, as most of the students recognized.

The second possible answer, the French National Assembly, contained far more than three parties both before and after World War II. In spite of this, many students, especially those in the lowest two-fifths, found this choice attractive. Only three of the highest group selected it, however. The Italian Chamber of Deputies should also be rejected as a possible answer because, after Mussolini came to power in 1924, it became less and less important until, in 1938, it was superseded by a Chamber of Fasci and Corporations and political parties were suppressed. This choice attracted only five or six students in each of the fifths.

Over half of the group of college students who attempted this question selected the correct response, the British House of Commons. Party A, on the graph, corresponds to the Conservative Party, Party B to the Labor Party, and Party C to the Liberal Party. The large Conservative majorities of 1924 and 1931 are clearly shown, as is the attainment of a majority by the Laborites in 1945.

Question 3

"In a flash it came upon me that *there* was the reason for advancing poverty with advancing wealth. With the growth of population, land grows in value, and the men who work it must pay more for the privilege. In allowing one man to own the land on which and from which other men live, we have made them his bondsmen in a degree which increases as material progress goes on. This is the subtle alchemy that in ways they do not realize is extracting from the masses in every civilized country the fruits of their weary toil."

The person most likely to have written these words is
(A) John Jacob Astor
(B) William Jennings Bryan
(C) Thorstein Veblen
(D) Lincoln Steffens
(E) Henry George

Statistical Analysis

RESPONSES	Students Classified by Total Test Score				
	LOWEST FIFTH	NEXT LOWEST FIFTH	MIDDLE FIFTH	NEXT HIGHEST FIFTH	HIGHEST FIFTH
Omit	32	22	15	16	4
A	5	6	2	1	
B	15	13	22	10	9
C	7	10	13	12	16
D	8	8	9	8	4
*E	6	15	13	27	41
Total	73	74	74	74	74

Per cent of total group of 369 students answering correctly . . . 28%
Correlation between success on this question and total score on test .47

(Discrepancies in total numbers in each fifth are caused by drop-out of students not completing the test.)

This question presents the student with a quotation and asks him to identify the person most likely to have made the statement. Note that the student is *not* asked to, or expected to, recognize the statement from memory. Instead, he is expected to read the excerpt carefully, to evaluate it in terms of his knowledge and understanding of American intellectual history, and then to select from the five names listed the person to whom the statement might most reasonably be attributed.

Some interesting results may be seen by examining the statistics obtained when the question was administered in a college-level American

*Correct answer

history test to a group of very able high school seniors. Because the question was a difficult one for the group, many students chose not to answer it at all rather than risk being penalized for an incorrect guess. This helped to differentiate between the able students and the less able ones. Whereas 32 of the students in the lowest fifth omitted the question, only four of the students in the top fifth did so.

Choice (A) served to attract only a few of the less able students. None of the top group thought that the statement could have been made by John Jacob Astor. An entrepreneur of the early nineteenth century who built up a vast fur trading empire in the Pacific Northwest, Astor would most likely be associated with the opening up of the Oregon country. In this huge, unsettled region where land was then readily available, he would hardly have been concerned with the particular economic problem discussed in the quotation. Moreover, anyone who recognizes the name has no reason to associate it with reform.

Choice (B) is a more sophisticated wrong answer than is (A). The students who selected William Jennings Bryan as the probable author of the passage were undoubtedly aware of Bryan's reputation as "The Great Commoner" — the self-styled defender of the people against the "dictatorship" of Wall Street, their champion in the campaign for free coinage of silver. Although the last sentence of the quotation might be slightly reminiscent of Bryan's style, the particular ideas are not those exploited by an orator who made free silver a "cause célèbre." This answer, while attractive to some of the students in the lower two-fifths, was most popular with those in the middle fifth. This may be partly explained by its greater sophistication, but the fact that most of the lower group had already chosen to omit the question probably accounts for the failure of that group to choose (B).

Choice (C), Thorstein Veblen, served to separate the better students from the very best. Few of the poorest students chose Veblen, partly because of the reasons mentioned above, and possibly also because they may not have been familiar with Veblen. The brighter students may have been more familiar with his name and ideas or at least with the fact that he was a critic of the American economic system at the turn of the century. They did not know enough, however, to realize that Veblen was not concerned with the monopoly of land as a cause of poverty.

Very few of the top group were attracted to choice (D), Lincoln Steffens. Concerned primarily with the problems of the cities, Steffens is perhaps best known for his exposure of municipal corruption.

Henry George, the correct response, was selected by over half of those in the highest fifth, but only six of the lowest group chose this correct answer. Altogether only 28 per cent of the total group could answer the question correctly, for a thoughtful understanding of the ideas of Henry George was required. The statement did not contain any of the catchwords usually superficially connected with George, such as "single tax" or "unearned increment."

Question 4

In the following questions you are asked to make inferences from the data which are given you on the map of the imaginary country, Serendip. The answers in most instances must be probabilities rather than certainties. The relative size of towns and cities is not shown. To assist you in the location of the places mentioned in the questions, the map is divided into squares lettered vertically from A to E and numbered horizontally from 1 to 5.

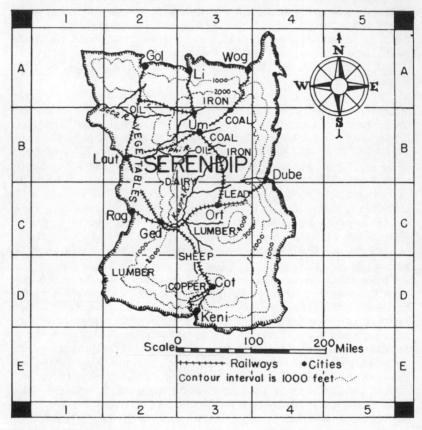

Which of the following cities would be the best location for a steel mill?

(A)	Li	(3A)
(B)	Um	(3B)
(C)	Cot	(3D)
(D)	Dube	(4B)

Statistical Analysis

| RESPONSES | Students Classified by Total Test Score | |
	LOWEST 27%	HIGHEST 27%
Omit	8	
A	10	2
*B	40	84
C	4	1
D	9	6
Total	71	93

Per cent of total group of 370 students answering correctly . . . 75%
Correlation between success on this question and total score on test   .43

(A somewhat different form of analysis was used for this test. Discrepancies in total numbers in each group are caused by drop-out of students not completing the test.)

A map of an imaginary country, such as that shown above, offers numerous possibilities for questions which measure important understandings. One could ask several questions requiring an understanding of the symbols used on the map. To determine student comprehension of the meaning of contour lines, for example, one might ask which railroad has the steepest grades to climb. Similar questions can be developed which require knowledge of the factors influencing population distribution, economic activities, and so on.

The question reproduced beneath the map requires knowledge of the natural resources used in producing steel and an awareness of the importance of transportation facilities in bringing these resources together. It was part of a general achievement test given to high school seniors.

The student who knows that iron is the basic raw material of steel and that coal commonly provides the necessary source of heat would proceed to locate deposits of these resources in relation to the cities listed in the question. He would be able to eliminate Cot immediately, since there is no iron or coal in its vicinity, although Cot might be an attractive choice to students who mistakenly think that copper is a basic ingredient of steel. Both Li and Dube are located reasonably near supplies of iron, and therefore might be attractive choices. Um, however, is the more clearly "correct" response, because not only are deposits of iron and coal nearby, but they are more readily transportable by direct railroad routes.

---

*Correct answer

Question 5

In the following question you are given a complete sentence to be rephrased according to the directions which follow it. You should rephrase the sentence mentally to save time, although you may make notes in your test book if you wish.

Below the sentence and its directions are listed words or phrases that may occur in your revised sentence. When you have thought out a good sentence, find in the choices A to E the word or entire phrase that is included in your revised sentence. The word or phrase you choose should be the most accurate and most nearly complete of all the choices given.

Although the directions may require you to change the relationship between parts of the sentence or to make slight changes in meaning in other ways, make only those changes that the directions require; that is, keep the meaning the same, or as nearly the same as the directions permit. If you think that more than one good sentence can be made according to the directions, select the sentence that is most exact, effective, and natural in phrasing and construction.

Sentence: John, shy as he was of girls, still managed to marry one of the most desirable of them.

Directions: Substitute John's shyness for John, shy.

Your rewritten sentence will contain which of the following?

(A) him being married to
(B) himself married to
(C) him from marrying
(D) was himself married to
(E) him to have married

Statistical Analysis

RESPONSES	Students Classified by Total Test Score				
	LOWEST FIFTH	NEXT LOWEST FIFTH	MIDDLE FIFTH	NEXT HIGHEST FIFTH	HIGHEST FIFTH
Omit	6	1	2		
A	4	2	5	1	3
B	9	6	2		
*C	9	21	33	44	45
D	11	8	3	2	
E	11	12	5	3	2
Total	50	50	50	50	50

Per cent of total group of 250 students answering correctly . . . 61%
Correlation between success on this question and total score on test .66

---

*Correct answer

In developing this type of question the committee of examiners reasoned that most good writers reconstruct sentences to change emphasis, to improve style, to avoid ambiguity, or to eliminate verbosity, and that the good student should be able to make such changes without involving himself in structural faults or grammatical errors. This type of question is designed, therefore, to assess the student's mastery of variety in sentence structure, his ability to make a change within a sentence so that it says what he intends to say more smoothly, concisely, and effectively than the original version may. Furthermore, the committee decided that to test this ability the question should require the student first to construct his new sentence mentally and then to compare his answer with a number of possible answers presented to him. As choices for answers they chose the kinds of expressions which students include in their own writing when they attempt to solve problems of sentence variety and become enmeshed in grammatical incongruities or verbal obscurities.

In order to select choice (A), a sentence like John's shyness with girls did not stop him being married to the most desirable of them would have to be used. To make this sentence correct, formal written English demands that the word being be preceded by the possessive pronoun his. Choice (B) presents a sentence similar to Despite John's shyness with girls, he managed to get himself married to one of the most desirable of them. This sentence is wordy and inappropriate in its tone (for formal English). Choice (C), however, yields a sentence on the order of John's shyness with girls did not prevent him from marrying one of the most desirable of them. This retains the meaning of the original sentence and contains no errors in grammar; it is the correct answer. The fourth choice might lead to John's shyness with girls did not keep him single; he was himself married to one of the most desirable of them. This sentence changes the meaning of the original sentence, and it is, at the same time, ambiguous in its own meaning. John's shyness with girls was not a reason for him to have married the most desirable of them — this sentence, an attempt to use the fifth choice, results in a complete change of meaning. It is therefore unacceptable, even though it is grammatically correct.

This question was answered correctly by 61 per cent of the college-bound high school students who attempted it. Most of the students in the two highest fifths answered it correctly, while a majority of students in the two lowest groups answered the question incorrectly.

Questions 6-7

The passage below is followed by questions based on its content. After reading the passage, choose the best answer to each question. Answer all questions following the passage on the basis of what is <u>stated</u> or <u>implied</u> in the passage.

Mill's estimate of Harriet's gifts may have been extravagant. Their contemporaries, few of whom knew her well, were inclined to question it. As Goldwin Smith waspishly remarked, "Mill's hallucination as to his wife's gifts deprived him of all authority wherever that came in." But
5 there can no longer be substantial doubt of the range of her influence. Mr. Packe corroborates the conclusion reached by Professor Hayek in his introduction to the Mill-Taylor correspondence — that Mill was only stating sober fact when he credited Mrs. Taylor (who later became Mrs. Mill) with a large share in the work published under his name. Nor was
10 it a matter of feminine flattery or, as Carlyle imagined, of "those great dark eyes, that were flashing unutterable things while he was discoursin' the unutterable." Mr. Packe insists that, except for the *Logic*, the principles underlying the more important works of John Stuart Mill were defined although not actually composed by Harriet Taylor, and that every
15 major work after the *Political Economy* was drafted or planned during their first few years of married life. This is not necessarily to accept Mill's view of his wife's mental endowments. She was obviously a woman of lively mind and exceptional charm to whom Mill responded intellectually as well as emotionally. But we may still suspect that her ascendancy
20 over him was, at bottom, one of those mysterious functions of personality rather than of intellect.

Question 6

According to Mr. Packe, Harriet's part in Mill's important works was
(A) mainly restricted to small details
(B) in the planning rather than in the execution of them
(C) in the comfort of her personality and charm
(D) only evident in the *Logic*
(E) helping with the more difficult sections

Statistical Analysis

RESPONSES	Students Classified by Total Test Score				
	LOWEST FIFTH	NEXT LOWEST FIFTH	MIDDLE FIFTH	NEXT HIGHEST FIFTH	HIGHEST FIFTH
Omit	4	11	4	2	1
A	1	3	1	1	
*B	19	34	51	46	64
C	14	8	5	11	4
D	22	6	3	2	
E	14	12	10	12	5
Total	74	74	74	74	74

Per cent of total group of 370 students answering correctly . . .   58%
Correlation between success on this question and total score on test   .51

Question 6 is fairly easy, and 58 per cent of a group of college-bound high school seniors answered it correctly. The question clearly asks for a re-statement of Mr. Packe's opinion as to the nature of Harriet Mill's contri-bution to her husband's work. In lines 5-9, we learn that Packe corrobo-rates Professor Hayek and John Stuart Mill himself in the view that Mrs. Mill had a large share in the work published by Mill. In lines 12-16, we learn that Packe considers this contribution to consist of plan-ning the work in outline. Accordingly, only (B) correctly states his opinion. Choice (A) is wrong because it suggests only a very small role for Mrs. Mill. Choice (C) fails to suggest any real intellectual contri-bution, which is counter to Packe's view that the principles underlying the works were defined by Mrs. Mill. Choice (D), which was the most popular choice of the least able group, states that Mrs. Mill's contribution is only evident in the *Logic*, whereas the passage reports that Packe spe-cifically excepted the *Logic* from his remarks. Finally, choice (E), while suggesting an important role for Mrs. Mill, goes far beyond the passage and describes her work as helping when difficulty arose. The passage nowhere suggests that she had such a role. The question correlates well with test score, as is evident from the increasing proportion of candidates who answer it successfully as the ability level increases.

---

*Correct answer

Question 7

This passage shows that Goldwin Smith's opinion of Mill was that Mill

(A) was naturally the person who would know best about his own wife's intellectual powers

(B) had no longer any authority over his wife

(C) was able by some sixth sense to see that his wife had outstanding intellectual ability

(D) was very seriously mistaken about his wife's intellectual prowess

(E) was not the real "architect" of the writings published in his name

Statistical Analysis

RESPONSES	Students Classified by Total Test Score				
	LOWEST FIFTH	NEXT LOWEST FIFTH	MIDDLE FIFTH	NEXT HIGHEST FIFTH	HIGHEST FIFTH
Omit	2	7	5	1	1
A	12	3	1	3	
B	27	29	30	22	23
C	6	5	5	2	
*D	8	12	16	36	42
E	19	18	17	10	8
Total	74	74	74	74	74

Per cent of total group of 370 students answering correctly . . . 31%
Correlation between success on this question and total score on test .48

Question 7 proved to be more difficult for the group (the two analyses are derived from the same candidates). It is much more specific, being based on the sentence in lines 3-4 which quotes the remark of Goldwin Smith. Smith, of course, is taking violent exception to Mill's opinion of his wife's gifts. He refers to this opinion as a "hallucination," and says that it deprives Mill of all "authority," i.e., all right to speak with authority, on that topic.

Clearly, then, the correct restatement of Smith's opinion of Mill is (D), which says that Mill was mistaken about his wife. Choice (A) is directly opposite in meaning, and is clearly wrong. Choice (B) is wrong, for it misinterprets "deprived him of all authority wherever that came in." It is the most common mistake, and many quite able candidates made it, but it is clearly wrong. Choice (C) is wrong in the same sense in which (A) is wrong: it is too positive a thing to say. Finally, choice (E) is wrong because it is completely beyond the scope of Smith's remark, which had nothing to do with the question of who planned Mill's work.

As in the first example, the question shows a definite tendency for the proportion of successful candidates to increase as the ability level rises.

*Correct answer

Question 8

In which of the following centuries was the piece of sculpture shown above most probably produced?

(A) The fifth century B.C.
(B) The fourteenth century A.D.
(C) The sixteenth century A.D.
(D) The eighteenth century A.D.
(E) The twentieth century A.D.

Statistical Analysis

RESPONSES	Students Classified by Total Test Score				
	LOWEST FIFTH	NEXT LOWEST FIFTH	MIDDLE FIFTH	NEXT HIGHEST FIFTH	HIGHEST FIFTH
Omit	16	9	10	5	3
A	6	7	9	7	6
B	9	8	1	5	
C	8	6	5	3	
D	5	3	5	2	3
*E	27	41	44	52	62
Total	71	74	74	74	74

Per cent of total group of 370 students answering correctly . . . 62%
Correlation between success on this question and total score on
   humanities section of test 40
(Discrepancies in total numbers in each fifth are caused by drop-out of students not completing the test.)

This question on art appeared in a test of general background given to college seniors and graduate students. To answer the question, the student must apply his knowledge of the characteristics of various periods in the history of sculpture in order to place the statue within its proper period.

The statue can be identified immediately as a product of western civilization because of its subject matter and design. The sculpture most commonly associated with western art in the fifth century B.C. is that done in Greece. During that period Greek sculpture showed its characteristic idealization of the human figure. If the student contrasts a well-known statue from that period, such as Myron's "Discobolus" ("The Discus Thrower") with the statue in the picture, he can easily discover that the treatment accorded the two figures is not the same. The figure of the woman pictured is not idealized, and although the frontal pose is found in Greek sculpture, a turned head on the figure is not. Therefore, choice (A) can hardly be correct.

In some countries sculptors of the fourteenth century A.D. began to create statues for use in palaces, chapels, and tombs of private individuals, but their work retained the qualities of the representations of saints found in the Gothic cathedrals of Europe. Statues of men and women associated with Christian history were also used as architectural decorations. In the fourteenth century probably only Eve would have been carved as a nude female figure, and she would certainly have been portrayed in a more modest pose and with a fig leaf. Although, like the figure of the woman pictured, the figures of this period of Christian art are not idealized, the

*Correct answer

statue of the woman displays none of the other characteristics of medieval art, and choice (B) can be eliminated.

The fifteenth century saw the beginnings of the Italian Renaissance, and by the sixteenth century sculptors were again presenting idealizations of the human figure, most often in a Christian rather than classical context. The statue pictured above shows none of the heroic character that is found in the works of Michelangelo and none of the exaggerated stylization that appeared in the works of his followers. Thus, choice (C) can be regarded as inaccurate.

Early in the eighteenth century sculptors frequently displayed a self-conscious coy femininity in their female nudes, but by the end of that century sculptors such as Canova had adopted the classical ideals and imitated classical models. Consequently, choice (D) is not a valid one, for the statue in the photograph does not resemble an eighteenth-century interpretation of a Greek goddess or nymph. It does, however, realistically present a human figure without any attempt at idealization. The realism here is thoroughly modern. The use the sculptor makes of texture points to the modern period, for it was only late in the nineteenth century that sculpture (such as Renoir's "The Washerwoman") used nonrepresentational texture as an integral part of the design and aesthetic effect of the work of art. Minor details in the statue such as the shape of the nose, the half-closed eyes (instead of open sockets), and the line of the hair indicate that the work is not classical in origin, and at the same time they point to the twentieth century school of art. The statue is actually "Junge Frau," the work of the modern German sculptor, Georg Kolbe.

The statistics show that the question was an easy one for the particular group that took the test. The correct answer was chosen by 62 per cent of the students. However, more of the students in the highest group than in the lowest group selected the correct response, and the incorrect answers were generally more appealing to the poorer students than they were to the better students.

Question 9

Directions: Maintenant, vous allez entendre une conversation entre deux personnes. Attendez la deuxième réplique et ensuite choisissez la réponse qui convient le mieux.

"Henriette, passe-moi cette petite robe légère qui se trouve dans mon armoire à glace."

"Attends un moment; j'ai la bouche pleine de pâte dentifrice. J'aurai fini ma toilette dans un instant."

(A) Ne te presse pas. Je la chercherai moi-même.
(B) Je l'ai trouvée tout à l'heure.
(C) Quand tu auras fini de te peigner.
(D) Oui, je l'ai repassée hier soir.

Statistical Analysis

RESPONSES	Students Classified by Total Test Score				
	LOWEST FIFTH	NEXT LOWEST FIFTH	MIDDLE FIFTH	NEXT HIGHEST FIFTH	HIGHEST FIFTH
Omit	3	1		1	
*A	21	29	45	57	59
B	14	4	1	2	
C	19	23	13		1
D	3	3	1		
Total	60	60	60	60	60

Per cent of total group of 300 students answering correctly . . . 70%
Correlation between success on this question and total score on test .65

The testing of a student's ability to understand a foreign language when spoken is a relatively recent development. Students listen to the recorded voices of native speakers in statements, short conversations, and short narrations. Suggested answers to questions based on the spoken material are printed in the students' test books. In listening comprehension tests the foreign language is used throughout, not only in the test questions but also in the directions to students. The sample question given here was part of a test designed for teachers of French in secondary schools. Paraphrased in English it reads:

---

*Correct answer

Directions: Now you will hear a conversation between two people. Wait for the reply of the second speaker and then select the reply which is most appropriate.

Recorded conversation:

"Henrietta, hand me the little summer dress which is in my closet."

"Wait a moment; I have a mouth full of toothpaste. I shall be through in a minute."

Answer choices:

(A) Don't hurry. I shall get it myself.

(B) I found it just a little while ago.

(C) When you are through doing your hair.

(D) Yes, I ironed it last night.

To select the right answer to this question, the student has to apply his knowledge of French grammar, vocabulary, and idiomatic expression, and his understanding of the French sound system. The students who have grasped the meaning of what they have heard will select (A) as the only choice that makes sense in the context. The literal use of the French word "trouver" (to find) in choice (B) misleads some who have not understood that the idiomatic expression "se trouver" in the conversation means simply "to be in a certain place." Choice (C) misleads those who have understood that the second woman will soon be finished with whatever she is doing but have not understood the nature of her activity. Choice (D) was selected by some students who mistook "passer" (to hand) in the conversation for "repasser" (to iron). This question was answered correctly by 70 per cent of those who attempted it. All but one of the top fifth selected the right answer, whereas only 35 per cent of the lowest fifth did so.

Question 10

One method of obtaining "artificial gravity" in a space station is to have the station rotating about axis AA' as it revolves around Earth.

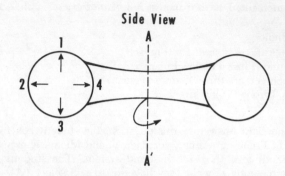

Side View

The inhabitants of the space station would call which direction "down"?

(A) Direction 1
(B) Direction 2
(C) Direction 3
(D) Direction 4
(E) Any one of the four, depending on speed of rotation

Statistical Analysis

RESPONSES	Students Classified by Total Test Score				
	LOWEST FIFTH	NEXT LOWEST FIFTH	MIDDLE FIFTH	NEXT HIGHEST FIFTH	HIGHEST FIFTH
Omit	3		1		
A		1		1	
*B	12	17	19	29	28
C	8	4	6	1	
D	7	9	6	3	6
E	4	3	2		
Total	34	34	34	34	34

Per cent of total group of 170 students answering correctly 62%
Correlation between success on this question and total score on test   .44

---

*Correct answer

This was part of a set of questions administered to high school students who were completing a year of high school physics. The question illustrates the kind of response that can be expected of well-trained students of high school age when they are presented with a relatively novel situation which is based on fundamental concepts from the field of mechanics.

This question requires that the student consider the nature of a possible mechanism for providing a "down" direction in a space station to simulate the gravitational "down" so important in our normal activities on Earth. Choice (C) is the direction normally considered down in diagrams. Although this direction is not significant in the space station, a sizeable number of the poorer physics students chose it. Other students assumed that the "down" direction would be that one toward the center of rotation of the station, choice (D). However, objects free to move in the space station behave as do particles in a centrifuge and "fall" to the outer edge. This direction, (B), then is the "down" direction in the rotating station. The other choices, (A), "up" as it is usually represented in diagrams, and (E), a direction which depends on the speed of rotation, were not selected by many students.

Questions 11-12-13

Questions 11-13 relate to the following information and graphs; they consist of five lettered answer choices followed by a list of numbered questions. For each question select the one lettered answer which is most closely related to it. An answer may be used once, more than once, or not at all.

A standard impulse is given at time t_0 to each of the several closed boxes having identical masses and identical appearance. The impulse starts the box into motion on a horizontal plane. There may or may not be friction (referred to as "external friction") between any box and the plane. It is known that each box contains a disk whose mass is equal to that of the box and which is resting on the bottom of the inside of the box. There may or may not be friction (referred to as "internal friction") between any disk and the bottom of its box. The disks may rebound in a perfectly elastic way from the walls of the box ("elastic walls"), or they may stick to the walls on colliding ("sticky walls").

The graphs below show the velocities of various boxes as a function of time.

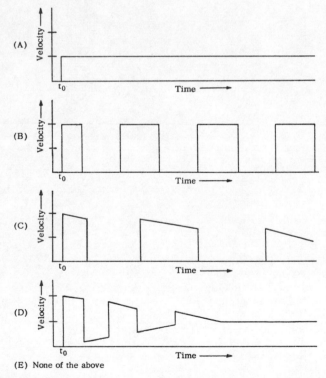

(A)

(B)

(C)

(D)

(E) None of the above

Question 11

Which of the graphs could represent the velocity-time relationship of a box that has no external friction and whose disk is fastened solidly to it?

Statistical Analysis

RESPONSES	Students Classified by Total Test Score				
	LOWEST FIFTH	NEXT LOWEST FIFTH	MIDDLE FIFTH	NEXT HIGHEST FIFTH	HIGHEST FIFTH
Omit	1	1			
*A	55	69	72	73	73
B	11	1			
C	2	1		1	
D	3	1	1		
E	2	1	1		1
Total	74	74	74	74	74

Per cent of total group of 370 students answering correctly . . . 92%

Correlation between success on this question and total score on test .56

This set of questions appears in one of the achievement tests developed to accompany the high school physics course of the Physical Science Study Committee.

Question 11 is the first of several questions based on the situation described. The series of questions requires a knowledge of certain aspects of kinematics and dynamics: an understanding of Newton's laws of motion and the concepts of velocity, acceleration, and momentum. The student must apply this knowledge to an unfamiliar problem and answer the questions in terms of graphs, a frequently used tool of the physical scientist.

The situation described is an idealized one since the complications of friction are occasionally ignored. The study of phenomena as they would occur under certain idealized conditions is a major way to attack complex scientific problems.

Question 11 pertains to a box with no external friction and with a disk fastened solidly to the box. When a standard impulse is given to the box with its attached disk at time t_o, the box would be set in motion. Since no friction or other force acts on the box after the initial impulse, the box would neither accelerate nor decelerate but would continue in motion at constant velocity. Choice (A) illustrates this motion.

The question was extremely easy; 342 of the 370 students (92 per cent) who attempted it answered it correctly. Nonetheless, the correlation between performance on this question and the test as a whole is high (.56).

The most discriminating incorrect answer choice was (B). Several students in the lowest fifth on the test seemed to recognize that in a frictionless situation, like that of this question, the velocity would not change with time, but they failed to recognize the simplicity of this situation and chose (B), where the velocity pattern is constant with time but where the velocity regularly drops to zero for short intervals.

---

*Correct answer

Question 12

Which of the graphs could represent the velocity-time relationship of the same box with external friction?

Statistical Analysis

RESPONSES	Students Classified by Total Test Score				
	LOWEST FIFTH	NEXT LOWEST FIFTH	MIDDLE FIFTH	NEXT HIGHEST FIFTH	HIGHEST FIFTH
Omit	2	2		1	
A	9	5	2	4	4
B	22	10	9	4	1
C	28	27	29	15	3
D	7	7	1	1	
*E	6	23	33	49	66
Total	74	74	74	74	74

Per cent of total group of 370 students answering correctly 48%
Correlation between success on this question and total score on test .70

One condition is now added to the situation described in the preceding question. The student is asked to choose the graph which could represent the motion of the box *with* external friction. The force of friction would act to decelerate the box and the attached disk at a constant rate. Therefore, the velocity-time relationship of the box would be:

Since none of the graphs given represents this motion, the answer is (E), None of the above.

This question was considerably more difficult than question 14; only 48 per cent of those who attempted it answered it correctly. One must determine what the velocity-time relationship would be and then recognize that the correct graphical relationship is not offered as a choice.

The correlation between performance on the total test and performance on this question is very high, .70. (B) and (C) were the most common choices of students with low scores on the test. These students apparently failed to realize that, as long as the disk is fastened to the box, the situation is as simple as if the disk were not present. The larger number of them chose (C), where the maximum velocity does drop with time, but both (B) and (C) have the weakness that they are appropriate only for more complex situations.

---

*Correct answer

Question 13

A box with elastic walls and no internal or external friction has its disk initially resting in the middle of the box. Which of the graphs could represent the velocity-time relationship of this combination?

Statistical Analysis

RESPONSES	Students Classified by Total Test Score				
	LOWEST FIFTH	NEXT LOWEST FIFTH	MIDDLE FIFTH	NEXT HIGHEST FIFTH	HIGHEST FIFTH
Omit	2	2			
A	17	10	5	4	
*B	18	28	44	53	69
C	15	10	6	4	1
D	16	17	16	11	2
E	6	7	3	2	2
Total	74	74	74	74	74

Per cent of total group of 370 students answering correctly 57%
Correlation between success on this question and total score on test .61

When the standard impulse is given to the box described in this passage, the box moves until the disk inside, free to slip along the bottom since there is no friction, hits the trailing end of the box. At this point, there is an elastic collision between the box and the disk, which have equal masses. All the momentum of the box is transferred to the disk, and as a result, the box stops and the disk moves across the bottom of the box. The disk soon hits the forward end of the box in a second elastic collision. The momentum is once more transferred to the box, the disk stops, and the box once again moves at the same velocity as before. The velocity of the box is undiminished since there are no frictional forces acting to slow the motions. Choice (B) represents this situation. This question was answered correctly by 57 per cent of the examinees. The correlation between performance on this question and performance on the total test in which it was used was high, .61. Only five of the students with the highest fifth of the test scores failed to analyze the situation correctly and to select the correct answer. Students with the lowest scores apparently did not understand the situation. Although very few of them omitted the question, their responses are distributed among choices (A), (B), (C), and (D) as if they were answering at random. Few of the students with the lowest scores chose the "None of the above" response, indicating their belief that the correct graph was presented, but they were, in general, not able to decide which one it was.

---

*Correct answer

Question 14

This question is based on the following situation:

A piece of mineral is placed in a bottle half-filled with a colorless liquid. A two-holed rubber stopper is then placed in the bottle. The system is then sealed by inserting a thermometer and connecting a glass tube to the stoppered bottle and a beaker of limewater as shown in the accompanying diagram:

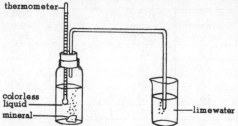

The following series of observations is recorded:

I. Observations during the first few minutes:
1. Bubbles of a colorless gas rise to the top of the stoppered bottle from the mineral.
2. Bubbles of colorless gas begin to come out of the glass tube and rise to the surface of the limewater.
3. The limewater remains colorless throughout this period of time.
4. The thermometer reads 20°C.

II. Observations at the end of thirty minutes:
1. Bubbles of colorless gas continue to rise in the stoppered bottle.
2. The piece of mineral has become noticeably smaller.
3. There is no apparent change in the level of the colorless liquid in the bottle.
4. The colorless liquid in the bottle remains colorless.
5. The thermometer reads 24°C.
6. The limewater is cloudy.

Which one of the following is the best explanation for the appearance of gas bubbles at the end of the tube in the beaker of limewater?

(A) The pressure exerted by the colorless liquid is greater than that exerted by the limewater.

(B) The bubbles coming from the mineral cause an increased gas pressure in the stoppered bottle.

(C) The temperature increase at the end of thirty minutes causes an expansion of gas in the stoppered bottle.

(D) The decrease in the size of the piece of mineral causes reduced pressure in the stoppered bottle.

(E) The glass tube serves as a siphon for the flow of gas from the bottle to the beaker.

Statistical Analysis

RESPONSES	Students Classified by Total Test Score				
	LOWEST FIFTH	NEXT LOWEST FIFTH	MIDDLE FIFTH	NEXT HIGHEST FIFTH	HIGHEST FIFTH
Omit		2			
A	10	4	3	5	1
*B	13	28	34	43	52
C	11	13	4	5	1
D	5		1		
E	21	13	18	7	6
Total	60	60	60	60	60

Per cent of total group of 300 students answering correctly . . . 57%
Correlation between success on this question and total score on test .55

This question is taken from a test designed to be used with a new curriculum in high school chemistry. The question is only one of a series based on the experimental situation described. Questions in the series are grouped in sequence relating to the situation in order to permit the student to think intensively in one setting for an extended period of time. The student is asked to deal with a realistic laboratory situation — one he has not yet encountered in the course at the time the test was given — and to employ scientific problem-solving ability in using the data given to answer the questions.

Choice (A) is both vague and irrelevant. It is unspecific about where the pressure is exerted and has nothing to do with the cause of the bubbles.

Choice (C) sounds plausible. In itself, the statement is not incorrect, since the temperature increase will cause an increase in gas pressure in the stoppered bottle. However, students who are in command of the subject will realize that the increase in gas pressure due to the rise in temperature is insignificant compared with that caused by the bubbles coming from the mineral.

Choice (D) embodies an incorrect statement. Some students may not realize this, but even if the statement were correct, it would offer an incorrect explanation for the appearance of the bubbles in the beaker.

Most of the good students rejected choice (E), but many less able students chose it, probably because the arrangement looks somewhat like a siphon and they had heard of the use of siphons in transferring fluids.

Students who understand the forces at work in the situation described will know that bubbles would appear at the end of the tube in the beaker when the pressure exerted by the gas from the stoppered bottle exceeded the pressure exerted by the limewater at the end of the tube. They will also realize that the limewater pressure would remain essentially constant. Choice (B), therefore, sets forth the condition that would account best for the appearance of gas bubbles at the end of the tube in the beaker.

---

*Correct answer

Question 15

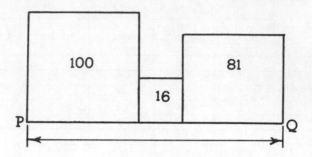

In the figure above, three squares with areas of 100, 16, and 81 lie side by side as shown. By how much must the area of the middle square be reduced in order that the total length PQ of the resulting three squares be 21?

(A) $\sqrt{2}$ (B) 2   (C) 4   (D) 8   (E) 12

Statistical Analysis

RESPONSES	Students Classified by Total Test Score				
	LOWEST FIFTH	NEXT LOWEST FIFTH	MIDDLE FIFTH	NEXT HIGHEST FIFTH	HIGHEST FIFTH
Omit	30	12	12	4	1
A	8	9	8	2	1
B	11	18	8	10	3
C	4	3	4	3	4
D	2	3	3	1	
*E	5	15	25	40	51
Total	60	60	60	60	60

Per cent of total group of 300 students answering correctly 45%
Correlation between success on this question and total score on test .66

This question is similar to those included in tests of mathematical aptitude for high school students. One of the problems surrounding such aptitude questions is the need to avoid familiar textbook material while at the same time restricting the content level to that which was mastered earlier in the junior high school — geometry and simple algebra. If this need is met, then the focus of the aptitude test is where it should be, namely on ingenuity in the solving of novel problems, rather than on the recall of memorized procedures. This ingenuity, or what some like to call "mathematical maturity," probably improves with taking good mathematics

---

*Correct answer

courses throughout high school but is not much affected by short-range cramming.

This question involves procedures which the student is extremely unlikely to have encountered in high school textbooks; the content knowledge required is certainly not beyond what is taught in the junior high school. The solution proceeds as follows:

> The lengths of the three sides of the squares are 10, 4, and 9, reading from left to right. Therefore, initially PQ equals 23. If the final length of PQ is to be 21, the amount of reduction of the side of the middle square must be 2. The middle square must consequently be reduced from an area of 16 to an area of 4; that is, it must be reduced by 12 square units.

Of the 59 college-bound high school students in this sample who omitted the question, 54 were in the lowest three-fifths. The 50 who chose (B) were students who started toward a correct solution but who stopped with the length of the new side of the middle square. The 18 choosing (C) seem to have proceeded as far in their solution as finding the new area of the middle square and, on the average, this was the most able of the groups missing the question. Choices (A) and (D) result from taking wrong directions in the solution of the problem and, as expected, these were selected by the least able groups.

Question 16

The question below is followed by two statements, labeled (1) and (2), in which certain data are given. In this question you do not actually have to compute an answer, but rather you have to decide whether the data given in the statements are sufficient for answering the question. Using the data given in the statements plus your knowledge of mathematics and everyday facts (such as the number of days in July), you are to select answer

- (A) if statement (1) ALONE is sufficient but statement (2) alone is not sufficient to answer the question asked,
- (B) if statement (2) ALONE is sufficient but statement (1) alone is not sufficient to answer the question asked,
- (C) if both statements (1) and (2) TOGETHER are sufficient to answer the question asked, but NEITHER statement ALONE is sufficient,
- (D) if EACH statement is sufficient by itself to answer the question asked,
- (E) if statements (1) and (2) TOGETHER are NOT sufficient to answer the question asked and additional data specific to the problem are needed.

If x is a whole number, is it a two-digit number?
- (1) x^2 is a three-digit number.
- (2) 10x is a three-digit number.

Statistical Analysis

RESPONSES	Students Classified by Total Test Score				
	LOWEST FIFTH	NEXT LOWEST FIFTH	MIDDLE FIFTH	NEXT HIGHEST FIFTH	HIGHEST FIFTH
Omit	11	6		1	
A	9	4	7	2	1
B	4	8	9	13	14
C	2	7	3	7	1
*D	11	19	30	24	37
E	21	15	11	13	6
Total	58	59	60	60	59

Per cent of total group of 296 students answering correctly 41%
Correlation between success on this question and total score on test .38

(Discrepancies in total numbers in each fifth are caused by drop-out of students not completing the test.)

One of the abilities which has been receiving increasing emphasis from the elementary school through college is that of judging the relevancy of

---

*Correct answer

data in the solution of problems in mathematics, science, and social studies. Measurement of the extent to which a student has developed this ability near the end of the high school years is believed to be important in predicting scholastic success in college. To accomplish such measurement the type of test question presented here has been designed, validated by research, and is now in use in the College Entrance Examination Board's Scholastic Aptitude Test. This type of question is used in arithmetic, algebra, and geometry. It shifts the emphasis from rote, manipulative skills to higher level judgments and reasoning.

This question shows the very great versatility of this type, for it requires little factual knowledge and the simplest aspects of elementary algebra, but does require a considerable degree of numerical judgment.

Fact (1) alone is sufficient because the square root of any three-digit square is a two-digit number. Fact (2) alone is sufficient because, whenever a three-digit multiple of 10 is divided by 10, the result is a two-digit number. The correct answer is therefore (D).

This question and its analysis provide an interesting insight into the functioning of this type of question. When the correct answer is (D), there is a sense in which the question becomes two questions, since two separate sufficiencies must be determined. In this case, when the sufficiency of Fact 1 is considerably more difficult to determine than the sufficiency of Fact 2, a certain number of moderately able people can be expected to choose (B) as the answer. One of the reasons that may have made the sufficiency of Fact 1 difficult for them to see is that although the square root of any three-digit number is always a two-digit number, the square of a two-digit number is not necessarily a three-digit number. The latter point may have led some to conclude erroneously that Fact 1 was not sufficient. Fact 2, on the other hand, can more easily be seen as sufficient because only a two-digit number can be multiplied by 10 to produce a three-digit number. The higher ability of the 121 selecting (D) is sufficient to give the question a good index of discrimination. The 20 choosing (C) apparently failed to realize that each of the two facts is independently sufficient.

Index

ABOUT THE AUTHORS

HENRY CHAUNCEY'S foremost professional interest lies in discovering methods for identifying each individual's abilities and helping the individual develop these abilities through an appropriate educational program. He has pursued this interest throughout three decades of activity in education and educational testing. A former school teacher and college dean, Mr. Chauncey's work as chairman of the committee on scholarships at Harvard contributed to the initiation of a special series of scholarship examinations, developed and offered by the College Entrance Examination Board. In 1942, these examinations became the College Board's admissions testing program. Mr. Chauncey has directed the activities of Educational Testing Service since this non-profit organization was founded in 1947 by the College Board, the American Council on Education, and the Carnegie Foundation for the Advancement of Teaching.

JOHN DOBBIN also came to testing from teaching and he has as his own major professional interest: "a preoccupation with the *ends* of education—its goals, its objectives, its output, its 'product'." Mr. Dobbin did his college and graduate work at the University of Minnesota, taught English and science at a Wisconsin high school, and later became test editor with a Minneapolis publishing house. Since joining Educational Testing Service in 1950, Mr. Dobbin has served as program director for the College Board's admissions testing program. He now lives in Florida where he devotes full time to writing, research, and work on special projects for ETS.